Crisis Management Strategy of the Prophet (ﷺ)

Prof Javed Iqbal Saani

PhD, MBA (MIS), MBA (Finance), BBA

Intellectual Capital Enterprise Limited, London

Copyright © 2022 Prof Javed Iqbal Saani

All rights reserved.

No reproduction of the book in any form such as electronic, photocopying, scanning, recording or otherwise. It also includes storing for retrieval purpose or transmitting through electronic media i.e., email. Prior written permission of the publisher may require doing any of the above under the relevant act that follows the Copyright, Design, and Patent Act 1988.Authors and the publisher are not responsible for any damage caused by the application/use of the concepts, techniques, instruction, or actions. The authors and publisher refuse any implied warranties or related matters.

Published by Intellectual Capital Enterprise Limited, ICE Kemp House, 152-160 City Road, London, EC1V 2NX; Printed in England with the collaboration of Amazon.co.uk.

Contents

About the author … vii

Dedication … xv

Acknowledgment … xvii

Preface … xix

1 UNDERSTNADING CRISIS MANAGEMENT … 23

Introduction … 24

Theoretical perspective of crisis management … 25
    Contingency Theory … 25

Crisis management model to follow … 26

2 SIGNAL DETECTION … 29

Introduction … 30

Identification of warning signs … 30
    Warning of Warqa bin Nofal … 30
    The Prophet (ﷺ) predicted migration to Madinah … 31
    Conspiracy of Quraysh … 31
    The Tabuk campaign … 32
    The battle of trench … 34

3 PROBING AND PREVENTION … 37

Introduction … 38

Active search … 38

Preparation/Prevention	40
1- Crisis: The Hijrah expedition	40
2- Crisis: The campaign of Tabuk	42
3-Crisis: The battle of Trench	45
Prevention: The treaty of Hodhabia	47
Background	47
The event	47

4 DAMAGE CONTAINMENT   51

Introduction	52
The battle of Uhad	52
The conquest of Makkah	53
Abu Sufyan visited the Muslim camp	54

5 RECOVERY   57

Introduction	58
Recovery from the battle of Uhad	62
Plan of the battle	62
Turning around	63
Counterattack	65

6 LEARNING   69

Introduction	70
The treaty of Hodhabia	70
Clarification of his mission	72
Initiating peace talks	72
Avoided the mischievous of Quraysh	73
The expedition of Hijrah	73
Organisational matters	74
Personal qualities	75
The conquest of Makkah	77

Reflection/critical analysis   78

7 CRISIS MANAGEMENT PLANNING   81

Introduction   82

Treaties with various tribes   82

Information Management   84

Planning for the battle of Trench   85

Planning for the battle of Uhad   88

8 CASE STUDY: THE CRISIS MANAGEMENT IN THE BATTLE OF UHAD   93

Introduction   94

The case in question   95

Crisis management   97

Crisis: The battle   98

The threat   98

Method of resolution   98

The plan   99
    The result   100

9 CONCLUSION   103

The significance of Crisis Management (CM)   104

Common factors   104
    Crises are commonplace   105
    Evolve in phases   105
    Management plans and effective communication   105

Concluding remarks   106

BIBLIOGRAPHY 107

INDEX 113

OTHER BOOKS BY THE AUTHOR (S) 119

Extension of Islamic Management Style 119

Discovery of Islamic Management Theory 119

Investigations of related topics 120

Finding of Managerial Implications of Major Expeditions & Ideas 120

Consolidations of significant themes 122

Identification of Managerial functions 123

Specific topics 123

Management Sciences 123

General Interest 124

Books translated into Arabic 126

REFERENCES 129

About the author

Javed Iqbal was a resident of Rawalakot (AJ&K). He received his Ph.D. from the University of Salford and an MBA (Information Management) from the University of Hull. Previously Dr. Iqbal received BBA and an MBA (in Finance) from the University of AJ&K both with distinction. The University of Azad Jammu & Kashmir, Muzaffarabad (AJ&K) awarded him two gold medals for his educational performance. The government of Pakistan selected him for higher education and deputed him to the UK to complete his doctorate. The government of Pakistan awarded him $100, 000 for it. Professor Iqbal joined IQRA University Islamabad campus as an associate professor in 2006. He became the head of Department of Technology Management in International Islamic University Islamabad (IIUI) in 2012. Dr. Iqbal joined AKU (AJ&K) as a professor in 2015 and became the Dean Faculty of Management Sciences. He is associated with Cardiff Metropolitan University these days.

The Deakin University of Australia has ranked his article "Learning from a Doctoral Research Project: Structure and Content of a Research Proposal" as the best piece of research for doctoral students. The article gained 2922 reads (Downloads) as of January 2021 on ResearchGate. An international organization nominated Dr Iqbal for the Award of Distinguished Scientist for his research contribution. Professor Iqbal has published twenty-two research articles and more than sixty books so far. He has developed an interest in Islamic Leadership Style/theory recently, therefore, most of his work is about it.

Professor Iqbal has published in such International Journals while his books on various subjects are available on Amazon, details are available inside the book. You can reach him @ iqbalsaani@gmail.com

Value of knowledge

Say (to them, O Muhammad(ﷺ)): Are those who know equal with those who know not? But only men of understanding will pay heed. [Az-Zumar: 9]

Value of knowledge I

Anas (May Allah (SWT) be pleased with him) reported: The Messenger of Allah (SWT) (ﷺ) said, "He who goes forth in search of knowledge is considered as struggling in the Cause of Allah (SWT) until he returns." [At- Tirmidhi]. Abu Hurairah (May Allah (SWT) be pleased with him) reported: Messenger of Allah (SWT) (ﷺ) said, "Verily! The world is accursed and what it contains is accursed, except remembrance of Allah (SWT) and those who associate themselves with Allah (SWT); and a learned person, and a learning person." [At- Tirmidhi, Book 1, Hadith 478.

Value of Knowledge II

Abu'd-Darda' (رضي الله عنه) said, "I heard the Messenger of Allah (SWT) (ﷺ), say, 1.'Allah (SWT) will make the path to the Garden easy for anyone who travels a path in search of knowledge. 2.Angels spread their wings for the seeker of knowledge out of pleasure for what he is doing. 3.Everyone in the heavens and everyone in the earth asks forgiveness for a man of knowledge, even the fish in the water. 4.The superiority of the man of knowledge to the man of worship is like the superiority of the moon to all the planets. 5.The men of knowledge are the heirs of the Prophet's (ﷺ). 6.The Prophets (AS) bequeath neither dinar nor dirham; they bequeath knowledge. Whoever takes it has taken an ample portion.'" [Abu Dawud and at-Tirmidhi; Riyadh us Salihin, Hadith 1388, p. 211]

Qualities of good leader/manager

It was by the mercy of God that you were lenient with them (O Muhammad (ﷺ)), for if you had been severe and hard-hearted, they would have forsaken you. So, pardon them and ask (God's) forgiveness for them and consult with them upon the conduct of affairs. [Al-e-Imran: 159]

Qualities of good leader/manager I

Hadhrat Ibn 'Umar (RA) reports that Rasulullah (ﷺ) said "Three persons are such as will have no fear of the horrors of the Day of Judgement, nor they will be required to render an account. They will stroll merrily on mounds of musk until the people are relieved of rendering their account. One is a person who learned the Qur'an, merely seeking Allah (SWT)'s pleasure and therewith leads people in salat in a manner that they are pleased with him; the second person is the one who invites men to salaat for the pleasure of Allah (SWT) alone. <u>The third person is the one who has fair dealings between him and his master, as well as between himself and his subordinates</u>" [Quoted by Al-Tibrani in Al-Majam Al-Slaasa; Fazail-e-Amaal, Virtues of the Holy Qur'an, Hadith 36]

Qualities of good leader/manager II

Abdullah Ibn-e-'Umar Radiy Allah (SWT) 'anhuma narrates that a person came to Nabi (ﷺ) and asked: O Rasulullah (ﷺ)! How many times may I forgive my servant? Nabi remained silent. <u>The man asked again: O Rasulullah (ﷺ)! How many times may I forgive my servant? He replied: Everyday seventy times.</u> (Tirmidhi) Note: In Arabic, the figure 'seventy' is used to express too many in number. [Muntakhib Ahadith, p. 415]

Basics of Islamic Management

And by the Mercy of Allah, you dealt with them gently. And had you been severe and harsh hearted, they would have broken away from about you; so, pass over (their faults), and ask (Allah's) Forgiveness for them; and consult them in the affairs. Then when you have taken a decision, put your trust in Allah, certainly, Allah loves those who put their trust (in Him). [Al-e-Imran: 159]

Narrated Abdullah ibn Umar: A man came to the Prophet (ﷺ) and asked: Messenger of Allah! how often shall I forgive a servant? He gave no reply, so the man repeated what he had said, but he kept silence. When he asked a third time, he replied: Forgive him seventy times daily. [Sunan Abi Dawud: Hadith 5164]

Rasulullah (ﷺ) said; 'Whenever three people proceed on a journey, one of them should be appointed as the Ameer (leader) of the group. (Mishkaat) [Fazail-e-Hajj, p. 56]

Striving for the cause of Allah (SWT)

Narrated Abu Hurairah: A man from the Companions of the Prophet (ﷺ) passed by ravine containing a small spring of thirst-quenching water, so he was amazed by how pleasant it was. So, he said: 'I should leave the people and stay in this ravine. But I will not do it until I seek permission from the Messenger of Allah (SWT) (ﷺ).' So, he mentioned that to the Messenger of Allah (SWT) (ﷺ), and he said: 'Do not do so. **For indeed one of you standing in the cause of Allah (SWT) is more virtuous that his Salat in his house for seventy years.** Do you not love that Allah (SWT) forgive your sins and admit you into Paradise? Then fight in the cause of Allah (SWT), for whoever fights in Allah (SWT)'s cause for the time it takes for two milking of a camel, then Paradise is obligatory for him.'" [Jami` at-Tirmidhi: English translation: Vol. 3, Book 20, Hadith 1650]

Enjoining piety is a·sadaqah.

Sayyiduna Abu Dbarr (RA) narrated that Allah's (SWT) Messenger (ﷺ) said," With the beginning of morning, sadaqah becomes due on every. bone of each of you. So, every tasbih is a sadaqah, every tahmid is a sadaqah, every takbir is a sadaqah, enjoining piety is a sadaqah. All that may be replaced by two raka'at (Cycles) one offers for the salah of duha." [Mazahir-i-Haq (Translation & Commentary of MISHKA TUL MASAABIH), Hadith 1311, V. 1, p. 778.]

Greatness of Allah (SWT)

Allah (SWT), the Exalted *in the name of Allah (SWT), the Beneficent, the Merciful.* 1. All that is in the heavens and the earth glorifieth Allah (SWT); and He is the Mighty, the Wise. 2. His is the Sovereignty of the heavens and the earth; He quickeneth and He giveth death, and He can do all things. 3. He is the First and the Last, and the Outward and the Inward, and He is Knower of all things. 4. He is Who created the heavens and the earth in six Days; then He mounted the Throne. He knoweth all that entereth the earth and all that emergeth therefrom and all that cometh down from the sky and all that ascendeth therein, and He is with you wheresoever ye may be. And Allah (SWT) is Seer of what ye do. 5. His is the Sovereignty of the heavens and the earth, and unto Allah (SWT) (all) things are brought back. 6. He causeth the night to pass into the day, and He causeth the day to pass into the night, and He is the knower of all that is in the breasts. [Al-Hadidh: 1-6]

Allah (SWT) likes those who love one another. Yahya related to me from Malik from Abu Hazim ibn Dinar that Abu Idris al-Khawlani said, "I entered the Damascus Mosque and there was a young man with a beautiful mouth and white teeth sitting with some people. When they disagreed about something, they referred it to him and proceeded from his statement. I inquired about him, and it was said, 'This is Muadh ibn Jabal.' The next day I went to the noon-prayer, and I found that he had preceded me to the noon prayer, and I found him praying. "Abu Idris Al-Khaulani (May Allah (SWT) had mercy upon him) reported: I once entered the mosque in Damascus. I happened to catch sight of a young man who had bright teeth (i.e., he was always seen smiling). Several people had gathered around him. When they differed over anything, they would refer it to him and act upon his advice. I asked who he was, and I was told that he was Mu'adh bin Jabal (May Allah (SWT) be pleased with him) The next day I hastened to the mosque but found that he had arrived before me and was busy in performing Salat. I waited until he finished, and then went to him from the front, greeted him with Salam and said to him, "By Allah (SWT) I love you." He asked, "For the sake of Allah (SWT)?" I replied, "Yes, for the sake of Allah (SWT)". He again asked me, "Is it for Allah's (SWT) sake?" I replied, "Yes, it is for Allah (SWT)'s sake." Then he took hold of my cloak, drew me to himself and said, "Rejoice! I heard Messenger of Allah (SWT) (ﷺ) saying, *'Allah (SWT), the Exalted, says: My love is due to those who love one another for My sake, meet one another for My sake, visit one another for My sake and spend in charity for My sake"*. [Riyad as-Salihin: English book reference: Book 1, Hadith 382] (Muwatta Malik: English reference: Book 51, Hadith 15)

Dedication

To my parents who invested heavily for our education and remained engaged in prayers for my success and wellbeing.

Acknowledgment

Special gratitude is due to all those who helped me to compile the work. I am grateful to my family who spared me to embark on the project. They also supply valuable information which enriched the contents of this effort.

I am obliged to pay my gratitude to honourable faculty members of International Islamic University Islamabad Prof Dr Muhammad Bashir Khan (ex-Vice president and dean of the Faculty of Management Sciences), Dr Abdul Zahid Khan, acting chairman of the Department of Technology Management (Faculty of Management Sciences) Dr Zubair Sarfraz, Advocate Islamabad High Court, and Prof Habib Tabeti of the University Mustapha Stambouli of Mascara, Algeria for their encouragement and support for the work. May Allah (SWT) reward them for their contribution? Ameen!

Preface

All prayers to Allah (SWT), the exalted, slat wa slam to all the Prophet (AS) especially upon the last (ﷺ), mercy and blessings upon his noble companions. May Allah (SWT) bestow upon his forgiveness to the entire ummah and ummah of all the Prophets (AS). And all those who received the right guidance.

Crisis is a situation which may emerge suddenly and needs solution quickly. For example, a natural disaster or a battle. Humans can control them to some extent but many of them are not controllable. It has been a popular subject of intellectual discussion especially after huge natural disasters of recent past.

The author had found the topic in the biography of the Prophet (ﷺ) a couple of years ago when he published "Management Practices of the Prophet". However, it was only a chapter in the treatise and was useful to expand it to the size of a book. Therefore, book is in your hands with the grace of Allah SWT.

The book has eight chapters. The first one introduces the topic. The purpose was to find out the meaning of the term "Crisis Management" and a model for analysis. The model consists of five phases. Thus, following five chapters describe them. Planning crisis was a key issue to prevent or minimise the impacts of crisis which needed a separate chapter. Therefore, chapter seven deals with it. The closing chapter describes a case study to cater the needs of teachers and students to understand the topic in real life situation.

The message of the book is to know that the Prophet (ﷺ) had managed crisis successfully. The topic is a part of Islamic Management Theory which the author had discovered recently. It is the forty third treatise on the subject with the grace and favour of Almighty Allah SWT. May Allah SWT accepts it. Ameen!

In general, my purpose is to pick up the qualities of our Prophet (ﷺ) and fit them to various aspects of leadership as managers understand them in the contemporary world.

I pray to Allah (SWT), the Exalted, to accept the humble effort and make it a source of forgiveness for me and the entire ummah. May it be a source of guidance for readers. Ameen! The author welcomes any suggestions to incorporate them in the future editions.

Prof Javed Iqbal Saani, Ph.D.

Manchester 13 September 2022

1 UNDERSTNADING CRISIS MANAGEMENT

Introduction

The topic is concerned with management of sudden or unexpected events which could cause harm to an organisation. It creates threats for the management and impede the achievement of their objectives. Sometimes it challenges the existence of the organisation. It suggests that the organisation must manage it to avoid its dysfunctional impacts on the reputation and envisioned objectives.

What is crisis?

The lingual definition of crisis is "a time of intense *difficulty* or danger." "a time when a difficult or crucial decision must be made." According to Collin dictionary "A crisis is a situation in which something or someone is affected by one or more very serious *problems*." In addition, crisis is "An unstable period, especially one of extreme trouble or *danger* in politics, economics, etc."[1] It suggests there are three key elements in a crisis:

- Danger
- Difficulty
- Problem

Let us define them so that we can design a model to address the case study of Uhad.

Danger is defined as a <u>possibility that something harmful or unpleasant will happen</u>, or a person or thing that causes harm.[2] Difficulty means "the quality or state of being hard to do, deal with, or understand : the quality or state of being difficult"[3] Also a difficulty refers to <u>something that hinders you or causes you to have to face challenges</u>".[4] Problem "is <u>something that has to be solved</u> or an unpleasant or undesirable condition that needs to be corrected."[5] We can conclude out of the discussion that danger is the possibility that something harmful or unpleasant will happen, difficulty refers to something that hinders you or causes you to face challenges. And problem "is something that needs solution. Given that let us investigate the case study to find out what danger (s), difficulty, and problem the prophet (ﷺ) had encountered and managed.

Crisis means "Crises of ..., confrontation with adversary groups and malevolent acts of governments, groups, and individuals." [6] Objective of "Crisis management is to protect an organization and its stakeholders from threats and/or reduce the impact of the threats."[7] According to Bundy and his colleagues "An organizational crisis—an event perceived by managers and stakeholders as highly salient, unexpected, and potentially disruptive—can threaten an organization's goals and have profound implications for its relationships with stakeholders."[8] This view is focusing on organisations at micro level or business organisation level. However, the earlies definition of crisis and key words stemmed out of it are broad in nature such as three key words: danger, difficulty and, problem.

Theoretical perspective of crisis management

There are many theories on the subject. An online source enumerated ten of them. These theories include contingency theory of management.[9] Let us see what it is all about.

Contingency Theory

Contingency means "the choice of an alternative course of action ... This means that the application of various management tools and techniques must be appropriate to a particular situation, because each situation presents a unique problem."[10] Contingency theory asserts there is no single best method to organize or lead a company, and that managers should make decisions contingent to the circumstances. Researchers say this applies equally in crisis management because crises are fluid, complex, and uncertain. Crisis managers must adapt their response to make it contingent upon the situation. It seems appropriate to investigate the crisis management approach of the Prophet (ﷺ) from contingency perspective. Iqbal Saani has examined the contingency theory in the discussion of theoretical contribution of the Prophet (ﷺ) to management theory elsewhere. [11]

Crisis management model to follow.

An online source describes five models for managing crisis. It includes Fink, Gonzalez-Herrero and Pratt, Burnett, Jacques, and Mitroff. All of them are practicable but we take Mitroff's model for this book because it is simple and associated with the circumstances of the situation i.e., applicable in Islamic perspective.

Mitroff offers a five-stage model for crisis management : "(1) signal detection, seek to identify warning signs and take preventative measures; (2) probing and prevention, active search and reduction of risk factors; (3) damage containment, crisis occurs and actions taken to limit its spread; (4) recovery, effort to return to normal operations; and (5) learning, people review the crisis management effort and learn from it."[12] We have investigated each of the stages in separate chapters i.e., 2-6.

Some related terms

It is important to understand some basic terms (related with synonym study) for the analysis e.g., danger, hazard, peril, and jeopardy. *Danger* is the general word for liability to all kinds of injury or evil consequences, either near at hand and certain, or remote and doubtful: to be in danger of being killed. The life of the Prophet (ﷺ) was in danger when the enemy encircled his home before leaving for Madinah. *Hazard* suggests a danger that one can foresee but cannot avoid: A mountain climber is exposed to many hazards. The Prophet (ﷺ) met several hazards during the journey of migration from Makkah to Madinah. *Peril* usually denotes great and imminent danger: The passengers on the disabled ship were in great peril. Muslims were in peril before the battle of Trench. *Jeopardy*, a less common word, has the same meaning as peril, but emphasizes exposure to the chances of a situation: To save his friend he puts his life in jeopardy. Abu Bakr (RA) jeopardised his life to save the Prophet (ﷺ) from an insect in the cave of Thore or Soar). [13]

2 SIGNAL DETECTION

Introduction

Signal deduction means "seek to identify warning signs and take preventative measures"[14] According to Bundy and his colleagues "An organizational crisis—an event perceived by managers and stakeholders as highly salient, unexpected, and potentially disruptive—can threaten an organization's goals and have profound implications for its relationships with stakeholders."[15] Given that we have examined a couple of examples from the life of the Prophet (ﷺ).

Identification of warning signs

Hijrah of the Prophet (ﷺ) and his colleagues was the first major milestone which changed the fate of the dawah responsibility and muslims. Here are some signals of the incident.

Warning of Warqa bin Nofal

Warqa bin Nofal was a knowledgeable person, when the Prophet (ﷺ) received the first revelation and meeting with the angel Gabriel (AS), Hazrat Khadijah (RA) took him to her cousin Warqa bin Nofal. Mubarikpuri describes the incident.

She set out with the Prophet (ﷺ) to her cousin Waraqa bin Nawfal bin Asad bin 'Abd Al-'Uzza, who had embraced Christianity in the pre-Islamic period, and used to write the Bible in Hebrew. He was a blind old man. Khadijah said: "My cousin! Listen to your nephew!" Waraqa said: "O my nephew! What did you see?" The Messenger of Allah told him what had happened to him. Waraqa replied: "This is 'Namus ' i.e. (the angel who is entrusted with Divine Secrets) that Allah sent to Moses. I wish I were younger. I wish I could live up to the time when your people would turn you out." Muhammad asked: "Will they drive me out?"

Waraqa answered in the affirmative and said: "Anyone who came with something similar to what you have brought was treated with hostility; and if I should be alive till that day, then I would support you strongly " A few days later Waraqa died, and the revelation also subsided.[16] It implies Waraqa informed (warned) in the early days of the Prophet (ﷺ) that he will have to leave his home town because his people would never allow him to live in peace.

The Prophet (ﷺ) predicted migration to Madinah.

Narrated Abu Huraira: Allah's Messenger (ﷺ) said, "I was ordered to migrate to a town which will swallow (conquer) other towns and is called Yathrib and that is Medina, and it turns out (bad) persons as a furnace removes the impurities of iron.[17]

When the pace of development of Islam slowed down in Makkah, the Prophet (ﷺ) sent two groups to Abyssinia to seek refuge and spread Islam. He also visited Taif, a nearby town where the tribe of Sakeef was living. The tribe was strong in number, and it had its own geographical territory. The purpose of the visit and the migration to Abyssinia was to find out an alternative place for the propagation of his idea in addition to other matters.

Conspiracy of Quraysh

Quraysh came to know about the plan of the Prophet (ﷺ) to leave Makkah and settled down in Madinah, a safe place for him and his companions. Therefore, they conspired for the assignation of the Prophet (ﷺ). Molana Kandhelvi described it.

"Hadhrat Urwa narrates that after the Hajj season, Rasulullaah (ﷺ) was in Makkah during the remaining days of Dhulijjah, Muharram and Safar. The Mushrikeen then gathered to conspire against him, thinking that he would soon be leaving Makkah since they knew that Allaah had created a place of safety and protection for him in Madinah. They had also found out that the Ansaar had accepted Islaam and that the Muhaajireen were going to them. The Mushrikeen, therefore, planned to capture Rasulullaah (ﷺ) and then either assassinate him, imprison him., exile him or keep him tied up. Allaah informed Rasulullaah (ﷺ) about their plot and revealed the following verse:

(0 Muhammad (ﷺ) Remember the time) When the Kuffaar schemed against you to imprison you, kill you or exile you (drive you out of Makkah). They plan and Allaah plans. Allaah is the best of planners." (Surah Anfaal: 30)

The day when Rasulullaah (ﷺ) went to the house of Hadhrat Abu Bakr (رضي الله عنه), Nabi (ﷺ) was informed that the Mushrikeen planned to assassinate him as he slept that night."[18]

Quraysh wanted to kill him because it was the viable way for them. Previous Prophets (AS) were also murdered by their nations. The ignorant people do not have any logical or ethical argument in the history of mankind against Prophets (AS). Force is and was the only alternative, so, Quraysh were thinking in the same way because they were illiterate and inconsiderate. The Prophet (ﷺ) responded because it was the right time for him to commence the sacred journey.

It signalled the Prophet (ﷺ) to know that a substantial threat is about to emerge which could put his life in danger.

The Tabuk campaign

The Prophet (ﷺ) received the news that the king of Rume is preparing to invade Madina i.e., the newly established Islamic state in the North. Lings describes the story with its background. He writes,

Not long after the battle of Hunayn the Emperor Heraclius had restored the Holy Rood to Jerusalem, and this marked the final fulfilment of the victory of the Byzantines over the Persians – the victory which the Revelation had predicted and of which it had said that day the believers will rejoice. 1 There was indeed cause for rejoicing that the Persians had been forced to evacuate their troops from both Syria and Egypt. But as regards Syria, one danger seemed to have been replaced by another. It was from that direction alone that the new Islamic state was threatened. There were growing rumours in Medina that Heraclius had advanced a year's pay to his army in view of a lengthy campaign against Yathrib. It was said, moreover, that the Byzantines had already marched south as far as Balqa' and had mustered the Arab tribes of Lakhm, Judham, Ghassan and 'Amilah. These reports were partially exaggerated and partially the reverse of the truth. It was not yet generally known that during the Persian campaign Heraclius had had a dream in which he saw the triumph throughout Syria of the kingdom of "a circumcised man", whom he had identified with the writer of the letter that had summoned him to Islam. The dream was of such power and clarity as to inhibit his movements towards the south and even his defence of Syria itself. He had now withdrawn from Jerusalem to Horns; and there, in his certainty that the whole province would eventually be overrun, he proposed to his generals that a treaty should be made with the Prophet (ﷺ), giving him the province of Syria on condition that beyond its northern frontiers there should be no further advance. Their amazement at this idea and their extreme aversion to it caused him to abandon it; but he never forgot his dream.[19] It suggests the Prophet (ﷺ) received the signals of a potential threat, consequently, he took defensive measures.

The battle of trench

Since the pagans of Makkah could not achieve their objectives in the battle of Uhad yet they planned to attack Madinah with the help of other tribes. It was due to the relative strength of Muslims compared to the previous military encounters. Mubarikpuri summarised the prelude of the event with its backdrop. He says,

The Jews, however, whose treachery, intrigues and disloyalty made them taste all types of humiliation and disgrace, were not admonished. After they had been exiled to Khaibar, they remained waiting anxiously for the results of the skirmishes going on between the Muslims and the idolaters. Contrary to their hopes, the events of the war were in favour of the Muslims, therefore they started a new stage of conspiracy and prepared themselves to deal a deadly blow against the Muslims, but were too cowardly to manoeuvre directly against them, so they laid a dreadful plan to achieve their objectives. Twenty chief the Jews with some celebrities of Bani Nadir went to Makkah to negotiate an unholy alliance with Quraish. They began to goad the people there to attack the Messenger of Allah promising them full support and backing. People of Quraish, who had been languid and proved too weak to challenge the Muslims at Badr, seized this opportunity to redeem their stained honour and blemished reputation. The same delegation set out for Ghatfan, called them to do the same, and they responded positively. The Jewish delegation then started a fresh effort and toured some parts of Arabia and managed to incite the confederates of disbelief against the Prophet (ﷺ), his Message, and the believers in Allah. Quraish, Kinanah and other allies from Tihama, in the south; rallied, ranked, and recruited four thousand men under the leadership of Abu Sufyan. From the east there came tribes of Banu Saleem, Ghatfan, Bani Murrah, etc. They all headed for Madinah and gathered in its vicinity at a time already agreed upon. It was a great army of ten thousand fighters. They in fact outnumbered all the Muslims in Madinah, women, lads, and elders included. To tell the truth, if they had launched a surprise attack against Madinah, they could have exterminated all the Muslims. However, the leadership inside the city was on the alert and the intelligence personnel managed to reconnoitre the area of the enemies and reported their movement to the people in charge in Madinah.[20] Thus, the news of the invasion was a serious threat to the community and the Prophet (☪).

We have referred five instances of reception of warning signals on separate occasions. We understand that it is the first phase of analysis of crisis. The next chapter takes the second step on the way the journey.

3 PROBING AND PREVENTION

Introduction

Probing and prevention mean "active search and reduction of risk factors" [21] According to the authors of the framework "The aim is to do as much as possible to <u>prevent crises</u> from occurring in the first place and to <u>effectively manage those which still happen despite best efforts</u>. The preparation/prevention stage includes creation of crisis teams as well as crisis training and simulation exercises."[22] Let us see the way of the Prophet (ﷺ) to manage various crisis situations. We have examined three instances of the issue in the following paragraphs.

Active search

Since the major source of threat which could generate a crisis was the Quraysh, yet the Prophet (ﷺ) was constantly watching their activities. He appointed Abbas (RA) for this purpose. For example. Abbas (RA) sent a letter to the Prophet (ﷺ) about the intentions of Quraysh. According to Mubarikpuri, "Meanwhile Al-'Abbas bin 'Abdul Muttalib, was closely watching the military movements and preparations for war, and these were all included in an urgent message sent by him to Prophet (ﷺ) who received it while he was in Quba' Mosque. Ubai bin Ka'b read the letter to the Prophet (ﷺ), who asked him to be reticent with respect to its serious contents."[23] Similarly, the Prophet (ﷺ) kept an eye on other circumstances. "Provocative actions continued and Quraish sent the Muslims a note threatening to put them to death in their own homeland. Those were not mere words, for the Prophet (ﷺ) received information from reliable sources attesting to real intrigues and plots being hatched by the enemies of Islam."[24]

The Prophet (ﷺ) captured news from the Ruman empire about its intention to have a military encounter. According to Lings,

There were growing rumours in Medina that Heraclius had advanced a year's pay to his army in view of a lengthy campaign against Yathrib. It was said, moreover, that the Byzantines had already marched south as far as Balqa' and had mustered the Arab tribes of Lakhm, Judham, Ghassan and 'Amilah. These reports were partially exaggerated and partially the reverse of the truth. It was not yet generally known that during the Persian campaign Heraclius had had a dream in which he saw the triumph throughout Syria of the kingdom of "a circumcised man", whom he had identified with the writer of the letter that had summoned him to Islam. The dream was of such power and clarity as to inhibit his movements towards the south and even his defence of Syria itself. He had now withdrawn from Jerusalem to Horns; and there, in his certainty that the whole province would eventually be overrun, he proposed to his generals that a treaty should be made with the Prophet (ﷺ), giving him the province of Syria on condition that beyond its northern frontiers there should be no further advance. Their amazement at this idea and their extreme aversion to it caused him to abandon it; but he never forgot his dream.[25]

Siddiqi believes that the Prophet (ﷺ) had sent many information gathering missions to various areas to find out movements of Quraysh. The purpose was to find out any crisis that may emerge. The Prophet (ﷺ) despatched a team of six person towards Makkah; they found a battalion of two hundred men in the command of Ikerma or Abu Sufyan near Senta al-Marah in Shawaal 1 AH. The team retuned; however, the enemy did not dare to do any mischief.[26] The Prophet sent another seven missions principally for the same purpose. It helped muslims to manage small expeditions and show their presence between Makkah and Madinah. It was a message for the enemy that muslims were alert and could encounter any crisis that may emerge.

Preparation/Prevention

1- Crisis: The Hijrah expedition

The migration was inevitable; therefore, it was a wise decision to get prepare for it. Iqbal Saani summarises the preparation for the event. The prelude of the crisis was the early arrangement.

According to Iqbal Saani, [27] If we look at the timing of it, it began long time ago. Prophet (ﷺ) went to the people of Yathrib in Mina during Hajj; invited them towards Islam and asked them that he needs a place where he could do his job peacefully. Molana Yousaf Kandhelvi writes in this connection,

Hadhrat Aa'isha (رضي الله عنها) says, "Every year Rasulullaah (ﷺ) used to present his case to the various Arab tribes, asking them to grant him asylum with their people so that he could propagate Allaah's word and message. He promised them Jannah in return for their assistance. However, no Arab tribe accepted his offer until the time came when Allaah decided that His Deen should become dominant, that his Nabi (ﷺ) should receive assistance and that His promises should be fulfilled. It was then that Allaah pulled forward the tribe of the Ansaar. They accepted the offer of Rasulullaah (ﷺ) and Allaah thus created a place to which Rasulullaah (ﷺ) could migrate."[28]

The Prophet (ﷺ) also sent his companions to Abyssinia for the purpose, and he travelled to Taif for the same reason, but he did not receive positive result from either of the sides.

We understand that the Hijrah was the outcome of the treaty that took place between the Prophet (ﷺ) and the Muslims of Madinah. Consequently, the Prophet (ﷺ) allowed his followers to emigrate to the new place. Most of them reached Yathrib before the Prophet (ﷺ) travelled.

However, the Prophet (ﷺ) was waiting for the Devine signal. Soon after it he commenced the preparations and planned the journey with the consultation of Abu Bakr (رضي الله عنه). Meanwhile, the pagans conspired for his assassination. Mubarikpuri has recorded the starting time; he states, "The Prophet (ﷺ) had thus left his house on Safar 27th, the fourteenth year of Prophethood, i.e., 12/13 September 622 A.D."[29] Similarly, he has taken some other steps to make mind for the event.

Allah (SWT) had decided the timing and Abu Bakr (رضي الله عنه) arranged the resources. Hadhrat Aiysha (رضي الله عنه) says, "Rasulullaah (ﷺ) said, 'Allaah has permitted me to migrate and to leave Makkah. Hadhrat Abu Bakr (رضي الله عنه), asked May I accompany you? Rasulullah replied, "Certainly," replied Rasulullaah (ﷺ). Hadhrat Abu Bakr (رضي الله عنه) said, "I have two camels that I have been rearing from a long time in anticipation for this day. You may take one." Rasulullaah (ﷺ) said, "Only at a price, Abu Bakr." Hadhrat Abu Bakr (رضي الله عنه) replied, "May my parents be sacrificed for you". You may have it at a price if you, so wish." [30]Thus, the required resources were available. The plan of the infidels to eliminate the source of guidance was about to fail. Allah (SWT) had a plan to eliminate *kuffer* from the sacred land forever. And it had happened after only a few years. Many of the prominent companions like Umer (رضي الله عنه) and Hamza (رضي الله عنه) already left. Ali (رضي الله عنه) and Abu Bakr (رضي الله عنه) were still in the native town. Abu Bakr (رضي الله عنه) wanted to emigrate, but the Prophet (ﷺ) asked him to wait.

Quraysh did everything to stop Muslims but failed. Lings states some details about the situation interestingly. He says,

"Quraysh did what they could to stop the emigrations. Suhayl's other daughter had now gone with her husband Abu

Hudhayfah, just as they had previously gone to Abyssinia, but Suhayl was determined that this time his son Abd Allah should not escape him, so he kept a close watch on him. Much the same happened to the son of the Sahmite leader 'As, Hisham, who likewise had been among the emigrants to Abyssinia. It was his half-brother 'Amr who had been sent by Quraysh to turn the Negus against the Muslim refugees, and Hisham had witnessed his failure and discomforting. 'Umar, who was Hisham's cousin - their mothers were sisters - had arranged that they should now travel to Yathrib together, leaving Mecca separately and meeting at the thorn-trees of Adat about ten miles north of the city. 'Ayyash of Makhzum was also to travel with them; but at the appointed hour and place there was no sign of Hisham, so 'Umar and his family went on their way with 'Ayyash, for they had agreed that they would not wait for each other. Hisham's father and brother had heard of his plan and held him back by force, and they put so much pressure on him that after some days they even persuaded him to renounce Islam."[31]

The companions were on the way to Yathrib despite all odds. Therefore, the Prophet (ﷺ) must join them.[32] We can conclude that the Prophet (ﷺ) had prepared for the event of Hijrah through which he prevented his companions from the persecution of Quraysh.

2- Crisis: The campaign of Tabuk

Background

The enmity emerged with Romans when they martyred the Muslim envoy Hazrat Haris bin Umair Azri (RA). In response, the Prophet (ﷺ) had sent a small contingent under the command of Zaid bin Harsa (RA) who fought with the battle of Mota. However, the strength of the opponents was still considerable.

The immediate reason of this battle was the threat of Romans to invade Madinah. Also, after the defeat of Quraysh most of the Arab tribes where in favour of the Muslims. New tribes were entering in the fold of Islam and other tribes were considering embracing the new religion. Mubarikpuri states the worry of Byzantine Empire,

> Caesar — who could neither ignore the great benefit the Mu'tah Battle had brought to Muslims, nor could he disregard the Arab tribes' expectations of independence, and their hopes of getting free from his influence and reign, nor he could ignore their alliance to the Muslims — realizing all that, Caesar was aware of the progressive danger threatening his borders, especially Ash-Sham-fronts which were neighbouring Arab lands. So, he concluded that demolition of the Muslims power had grown an urgent necessity. This decision of his should be achieved before the Muslims become too powerful to conquer and raise troubles and unrest in the adjacent Arab territories.[33]

To materialise these ambitions the Byzantines decided to initiate a decisive step to neutralise Muslim power. They gathered a large army with the help of their Arab confederates. At one point the enemy gathered 40,000 strong army and gathered in Belqa. It ignited the hopes of hypocrites of Madinah and surroundings. They wanted to eliminate Muslims as soon as possible at any cost. Therefore, they had constructed a separate place of worship so that they can conspire in privacy. It provided them a base camp for planning their malicious aspires. They were so much dare that they had invited the Prophet (ﷺ) to lead a prayer in the new place. The Prophet (ﷺ) postponed it till his return from the campaign.

The purpose of the Battle was to show Romans and others that Muslims were now a real military power in the area. The Battle would have completed the influence of Muslims in Arab lands; it was also a decent effort to control the hypocrites and others indeed.

Preparations

The Prophet (ﷺ) had recruited the companion from Medina, Arab tribes, and Makkah. In addition to the manpower, the Prophet (ﷺ) had contributed a lot of money and resources from Muslims to finance the army. He had appointed a deputy (Governor of Madinah) and deputed Ali (RA) for looking after his family. A substantial number of people gathered to accompany the Prophet (ﷺ).

On ground, the physical circumstances were very odd. It was extremely hot, people were threatened with famine and poverty, mounts were limited, the crops were ready and the journey was long. It restricted people to go immediately for the campaign.

Nevertheless, the Prophet (ﷺ) had taken a decisive decision to go out at all costs. He knew that the invasion of Byzantines would create bad image of Muslims, they could lose the advantages of the previous conquests. The possibility of revival of idolaters could not be ruled out.

As a result, the Prophet (ﷺ) had announced the expedition. He invited people of Makkah, the confederate tribes, and the inhabitants of Madinah. He inspired people for fighting for the cause of Allah (SWT) and motivated them for spending in the path of Almighty. The companions had contributed generously but there was lack of resources due to the considerable number of participants. Many willing to join the campaign could not accompany the troops because of unavailability of mounts. Usman (RA), Abdurrehman bin Ouff (RA), Abu Bakr (RA), Umer (RA), Abbass (RA), Talha (RA), Saad bin Ubaidhah (RA), Muhammad bin Musalmah (RA), Asim bin Addi (RA) were the prominent contributors. Women also took part enthusiastically in the collection.

Passionate tribes and people gathered quickly on the call of the Prophet (ﷺ). Lings described the movements.

> When all the Bedouin contingents had arrived, the army was thirty thousand strong, with ten thousand horses. A camp was made outside the town, and Abu Bakr was put in charge of it until, when all was ready for the march, the Prophet (ﷺ) himself rode forth and took command.[34]

The Prophet (ﷺ) had prevented an attack on Madinah through the campaign. His active preparation for it were proverbial because the campaign was known as the "the army of distress".

3-Crisis: The battle of Trench

It took place in the year five of Hijrah. Since Quraysh were unsuccessful in the battle of Uhad because they did not have enough strength, yet they invited other tribes to eliminate muslims for the new attack. The Prophet (ﷺ) had taken following measures to manage it.

Probing

It means "inquiring closely into something; searching." And probe means "seek to uncover information about someone or something."[35] The Prophet (ﷺ) and his advisory team was keeping an eye on the movement of enemy. Mubarikpuri reports the search for information so that a plan of action may be articulated about the situation. He says,

"The leadership inside the city was on the alert and the intelligence personnel managed to reconnoitre the area of the enemies and reported their movement to the people in charge in Madinah. The Messenger of Allah summoned a high advisory board and conducted a careful discussion of a plan to defend Madinah. After a lengthy talk between military leaders and people possessed of sound advice, it was agreed on the proposal of an honourable Companion, Salman Al-Farisi, to dig trenches as defensive lines."[36]

The rationale of the trench and preparations

The purpose was to find out a way to prevent the danger of enemy to attack on Madinah. The strategy was successful because the enemy hardly crossed over the trench. It saved the Islamic troops and the city.

There were many reasons of digging the ditch. It was a navel strategy under the circumstances. The number of enemy forces were far larger than their counterpart. Physically, "The northern part of Madinah was the most vulnerable, all the other sides being surrounded by mountains and palm tree orchards, the Prophet (ﷺ) as a skilful military expert, understood that the confederates would march in that direction, so the trench was ordered to be on that side."[37] Furthermore "Time was short and all efforts would have to be strained to the utmost if no dangerous gap was to be left in the defences. But the trench did not need to be continuous; at many places a long stretch of fortress-like houses at the edge of the city was adequate protection; and to the north-west there were some masses of rock which in themselves were impregnable and merely needed to be connected to each other. The nearest of these, known as Mount Sal', was to be brought within the entrenchments, for the ground in front of it was an excellent site for the camp. The trench itself would bound the camp in the north in a wide sweep from one of the rocky to eminences to a point on the eastern wall of the town. This was to be the longest single stretch of trench and the most important."[38] Thus, it protected the unguarded area of the city. Keeping these benefits, the Prophet (ﷺ) ordered the preparation of a ditch to protect the empty place from where the enemy could infiltrate after consultation with his "cabinet".

Prevention: The treaty of Hodhabia

We have discussed three instances of crisis. One of them was a non-battle situation while others were wars. Since Quraysh initiated wars yet it was difficult for the Prophet (ﷺ) to prevent them. Nevertheless, he had avoided a battle between the parties through the treaty of Hodhabia. Iqbal Saani described the event.

Background

There are several reasons for the selection of Hodhabia as a case for avoiding/preventing the battle. First, it was the non-fighting expedition of the Prophet (ﷺ). Secondly, he had avoided a war due to his vigilance and foresight. Thirdly, he had negotiated with Quraysh while previous encounters were armed 'meetings. The Prophet (ﷺ) had to manage his companions because of the conditions of the treaty which were defensive in nature. And the Prophet (ﷺ) was given glad tiding of 'disguised glory' in the apparent retreat. The Divine Will was with the Prophet (ﷺ). "The Hudaibiyah encounter occurred meanwhile that not only gave Muslims courage to go ahead with the mission, but it also tested their courage and faith in Islam."[39]

The event

According to Lings[40] one night towards its end he dreamed that with his head shaved he entered the Ka'bah, and its key was in his hand. The next day he told his Companions of this and invited them to perform the Lesser Pilgrimage with him, whereupon they hastily set about preparing so that they could leave as soon as possible. Between them, they purchased seventy camels to be sacrificed in the sacred precinct. Their meat would then be distributed among the poor of Mecca. The Prophet (ﷺ) decided to take one of his wives with him, and when lots were cast the lot fell to Umm Salamah (RA).

Consequently, he has announced in and around Madinah about his intention of performing Umrah. He appointed two companions as his deputy and marched towards Makkah in 6 A.H. with 1400 companions. He wore ihram and prepared animals for sacrifice at Zulhalifah (The boundary of harum from Madinah side).

He had also appointed an intelligence officer to know the possible reaction of Quraysh or other tribes. The officer informed him at Asfaan and described the plans of enemy tribes during the journey. They were getting prepared to stop the Prophet (ﷺ) on the way to his destination.

The Prophet (ﷺ) consulted his team and put forward two proposals: to fight with these tribes and clear the way to reach Makkah, or avoid them and continue the journey. He opted the later scheme. Meanwhile, the Prophet (ﷺ) came to know that Quraysh was also in fighting 'mode' and they had dispatched a squad of 200 horse riders under the command of Khalid bin Waleed through another intelligence source. Khalid was planning to attack while Muslims were supposed to pray salat. Allah (SWT) sent down the special order of praying in the battlefield. It restricted the enemy to take advantage of the opportunity. On top of that, the Prophet (ﷺ) changed his way to avoid any encounter with Quraysh. The path was difficult and rocky, but he continued till Hodhabia and encamped there near a small water well.

Tribes of Khaza was a confederate of Muslims, some of them approached the Prophet (ﷺ) and explained him the plans of Quraysh. Badheel bin Warqa informed him that they would never allow you to enter Makkah. The Prophet (ﷺ) said they were not there to fight but if they would be forced to do so "I swear to Allah that I will fight with them for the cause of my mission until I get martyred or they would be defeated".[41] Nevertheless, he put a peace proposal for them. Badheel conveyed the message to Quraysh who sent their ambassador for further conversation.

Both sides exchanged their views through representatives but without outcome because Quraysh was die-heart. They sent a group of 70/80 warriors secretly to attack Muslims to damage the peace talks. Muslims guards captured them, but the Prophet (ﷺ) released them as a positive gesture to continue peace efforts.

The Prophet (ﷺ) had deputed Usman (RA) to talk to Quraysh after consultation with others. He was selected because he was a respectable person of mild temperament, and his clan was still in Makkah. In case of an accident, his clan could help him out. The Prophet (ﷺ) advised him:

- Tell them that we are peaceful.
- Invite them to Islam
- Give glad tiding to the Muslim still living in Makkah about the dominance of Islam in Makkah soon.

Usman (RA) conveyed the message of the Prophet (ﷺ) to the key figures of Quraysh. They offered him to do tawaf of Kaaba, but he refused. Quraysh asked him to stay a little bit more so that they could decide about the outcome of the conversation.

Meanwhile, a rumour reached the Prophet (ﷺ) that Quraysh had martyred Usman (RA). The Prophet (ﷺ) reacted quickly and asked his companions to get prepare for a battle. He took famous pledge known in the Islamic history as "Bait-e-Rizwaan". It was the pledge of the fight for the cause of Allah (SWT) and to remain steadfast in the battlefield. However, soon after it, Usman (RA) returned, and he took the same as well.

Quraysh received the message and immediately sent their mediator. The competing parties arrived at a truce at last. Some conditions were against the Muslims but other conditions provided them strength. Quraysh accepted Islam as a force/party which compelled them to allow Muslims to do Umrah the following year.

Allah (SWT) gave glad tidings of victory to the Prophet (ﷺ). Muslims officially included their confederate (i.e., Banu Khaza) in their ranks. Doors opened to other tribes to join hands with Muslims. The treaty offered a decade of peace for them. Peace always supports Muslim cause because it provides an opportunity for Muslims to present their message to others. War used to be a source of bloodshed that increases the gulf of hatred. It creates a communication gap that hinders non-Muslims to study and understand Islam.

Muslims were under moral pressure when Abu Jandal (RA) arrived and solicit the help of the Prophet(ﷺ). The Prophet (ﷺ) tried to settle down his matter, but the negotiator was his father who was not ready at any cost to leave him with Muslims. The Prophet (ﷺ) advised him, "be patient". He said to the nearest effect that Allah (SWT) would open a door of salvation for you and all those who were suffering from the hands of infidels.

Thus, the Prophet (ﷺ) had prevented a battle with the truce and gained the access to the holy city. It had numerous advantages to Muslims as we have described in the above paragraphs.

4 DAMAGE CONTAINMENT

Introduction

According to Mitroff "The intent of the third phase, damage containment, is to limit the effects. Effective management of this phase would detail plans for preventing a localized crisis from affecting other uncontaminated parts of the organization or its environment."[42] Some crises may be managed partially, fully, or not at all. It means the organisation must sustain the damage. There were a few situations where the Prophet (ﷺ) had managed such situations.

The battle of Uhad

The notable event was the battle of Uhad. The Prophet (ﷺ) appointed a band of fifty archers on a specific entry point from where the enemy could attack. Muslims gained upper hand in the beginning of the battle; thus, the band left its position because they perceived the Muslims achieved victory. But the fight was still in progress. Meanwhile the enemy initiated a flank attack from the same place where the Prophet (ﷺ) stationed the band.

Muslim army received upper hand in the beginning but encountered sever resistance from the enemy in the later phase of the battle. It was due to the flank attack of the opposition. However, the Prophet (ﷺ) had adopted a defensive strategy which kept the loss at its minimum. Mubarikpuri believes that the battle was a draw because none of the parties claimed victory. For instance, Muslims had upper hand in the start but sustained losses in the middle part of the fight. Muslims gathered at one place around the Prophet (ﷺ) while defending their position successfully.

The expert of war used to measure the success of an army/battle in several ways during that time. First, the opponent used to flee from the battlefield, the victorious used to collect the spoils of war and the winner used to stay at the place of battle for 2/3 days to show their success. For example. the Prophet (ﷺ) distributed the spoils of war among soldiers after the victory of Badr. However, Quraysh had not done any of these. They neither stayed in the battlefield for even a day nor distributed spoils of war.

In addition, the Prophet (ﷺ) followed them to a place called Hamra-Al-Asad. Muslim army stayed there for three days in the anticipation that Quraysh might return to reattack, but they could not dare to do so. It was partially due to an envoy which the Prophet (ﷺ) had dispatched to discourage Quraysh for reattack. [43] It suggests that they inflict human loss to Muslims but could not win the battle. When an army wins a war, it did not reattack because they did not need it.

Thus, the Prophet's (ﷺ) plan to go to Hamra-Al-Asad prevented the enemy to cause more damage to Muslims. If they would have returned and initiate fight, it could involve more loss of human lives and military assets. Moreover, the steadfastness of Muslim army discouraged Quraysh to attack on the city of Madinah during the battle of Uhad because the city was empty of military personnel.

The conquest of Makkah

The plan of the Prophet (ﷺ) was to avoid/minimized bloodshed. He took a couple of measures for it. First, he wanted to reach Makkah suddenly so that Quraysh could not prepare for a fight. He made supplication to Allah SWT to keep the matter secret. However, a companion sent a letter to his family about the intentions of Muslims. Allah SWT informed the Prophet (ﷺ) about it and Muslims recovered the letter from a woman. Ibn Ishaq describes the event,

"When the apostle decided to go to Mecca Hatib b. Abu Balta'a wrote a letter to Quraysh telling them that the apostle **intended to come at them. He gave it to a woman whom Muhammad b.** Ja'far alleged was from Muzayna while my other informant said she was Sara, a freed woman of one of the B. 'Abdul-Muttalib. He paid her some money to carry it to Quraysh. She put the letter on her. head and then **plaited her locks over it and went off. The apostle received news from** heaven of Hatib's action and sent 'Ali and al-Zubayr b. al-'Awwam with instructions to go after her. They overtook her in al-KhuIayqa of B. Abu Ahmad. They made her dismount and searched her baggage but found nothing. 'Ali swore that the apostle could not be mistaken nor could they, and that if she did not produce the letter, they would strip her. When she **saw that he was in earnest she told him to turn aside, and then she let down** her locks and drew out the letter and gave it to him and he took it to the apostle."[44]

Abu Sufyan visited the Muslim camp.

Although Abu Sufyan accepted Islam the day before the march of Muslims towards Makkah, but he was still the chief of Quraysh. The Prophet (☪) wanted him to impress with the number of soldiers he was leading so that he must tell the people of Makkah that they are unable to combat with Muslim army. So, it is better to lay the arms down. The Prophet (☪) asked Abbass (RA) to stand with Abu Sufyan on the side from where the muslims army supposed to pass by. Lings captured the scene.

The tents had already been loaded on to the transport camels, and the Prophet (☪) had at last called for the standards and pennants, to be brought to him. These he mounted one by one, placing each in the hand of the bearer he had chosen for it. He told 'Abbas to accompany Abu Sufyan as far as the narrow end of the valley, and keep him there, so that he could see for himself the size of the army as it passed. There would be time enough for him then to return to Quraysh and deliver his message, for a single man could reach Mecca by a more direct way than the army would take. "Who is that?" said Abu Sufyan, pointing to the man at the head of the host which now came insight. "Khalid the son of Walid," said 'Abbas; and when he came level with them Khalid uttered three magnifications, Allahu Akbar. With Khalid were the horse of Sulaym. They were followed by the yellow-turbaned Zabayr at the head of a troop of five hundred Emigrants and others. He likewise uttered three magnifications as he passed Abu Sufyan, and the whole valley resounded as with one voice his men echoed him. Troop after troop went by, and at the passing of each Abu Sufyan asked who they were, and each time he marvelled, either because the tribe in question had hitherto been far beyond the range of influence of Quraysh, or because it had recently been hostile to the Prophet (ﷺ), as was the case with the Chatafanite clan of Ashja', one of whose ensigns was borne by Nu'aym, the former friend of himself and Suhayl. "Of all the Arabs," said Abu Sufyan, "these were Muhammad's bitterest foes." "God caused Islam to enter their hearts," said 'Abbas. "All this is by the grace of God."[45] The magnificent sight of the Muslim army impressed Abu Sufyan who according to Mubarikpuri, "Abu Sufyan began to wonder who those people were, to which Al-'Abbas told him that they were Muhammad and his Companions. Abu Sufyan said that no army however powerful could resist those people and addressing Al-'Abbas, he said: "I swear by Allah that the sovereignty of your brother's son has become too powerful to withstand." Al-Abbas answered, "It is rather the power of Prophethood," to which the former agreed."[46] Having seen the marvels power of the Prophet (ﷺ) "Al-Abbas urged Abu Sufyan to hasten into Makkah and warn the Quraishes against any aggressive behaviour towards the Muslims. There in Makkah, he shouted at the top of his voice and warned against any hostilities advising them to seek safety in his house. His wife got indignant and tugged at his moustache cursing him and abusing his cowardly stance. The people within Makkah mocked Abu Sufyan and dispersed in different directions, some into their houses, others into the Holy Sanctuary while some undisciplined reckless ruffians led by 'Ikrimah bin Abi Jahl, Safwan bin Omaiyah and Suhail bin Amr encamped themselves in a place called Khandamah, with a murderous intent in their minds." [47]

At another part of the mount 'Ikrimah, Safwan and Suhayl had gathered a force of Quraysh together with some of their allies of Bakr and Hudhayl. They were determined to fight; and when they saw Khalid's troop making for the lower entrance to the city they came down and attacked them. But they were no match for Khalid and his men, who put them to flight, having killed some thirty of them with the loss of only two live son their own side. 'Ikrimah and Safwan escaped on horseback to the coast; Suhayl went to his house and locked the door.[48]

The Prophet (ﷺ) wanted to minimize the loss of human lives, but he said about the incident that "It was distained". Nevertheless, the Prophet (ﷺ) minimized the damage to achieve his objective. He adopted the strategy of keeping the entire campaign secret and called Abu Sufyan to see the strength of Muslim army to discourage him for fighting.

5 RECOVERIES

Introduction

Recovery means "the regaining or returning of something ... A return to former status ... A regaining of balance, control, composure, etc."[49] When we look at some crises the Prophet (☬) had encountered such as the intention of Umrah before the treaty of Hodhabia, the Prophet (☬) attained the recovery after abandoning Umrah. It was following the conditions of the truce; thus, muslims supposed to do Umrah the following year. The Prophet (☬) gained control of the situation during the battle of Uhad when Muslims gathered at a given place with the Prophet (☬). Here are some details of these events.

Recovery from the Treaty of Hodhabia

Muslims encamped in Hudaybiyah before entering the holy precent; Quraysh came to know about them and sent their envoy who informed the Prophet (☬) about the intentions of Quraysh,

One of their leading men, Budayl ibn Warqa', was in Mecca when news came that the pilgrims were encamped at Hudaybiyah. He now went with some of his clansmen to the Prophet (☬) to inform him of the attitude of Quraysh. "They swear by God," he said, "that they will not leave the way open between thee and the House until the last of their fighting men hath perished." The Prophet (☬) said: "We came not here for battle; we came only to make our pilgrimal rounds about the House. He that standeth in our way, him we shall fight; but I will grant them time, if they so desire it, to take their precautions and to leave the way clear for us."[50]

However, the Prophet (☬) settled the crisis through a lengthy process of negotiation. Iqbal Saani writes about the concept of negotiation as

"It is a process of give and take to arrive at a conclusion or agreement. "It's often said that great leaders are great negotiators." The dictionary defines it as "the process of discussing something with someone in order to reach an agreement with them, or the discussions themselves." According to a CIMA writer, negotiation is "The process through which two or more parties who are in conflict over outcomes try to reach agreement. It is the constructive, positive alternative to haggling or arguing; it is aimed at building an agreement rather than winning a battle." Hodhabia was a complicated agreement which entails compromising with the opponents and satisfying colleagues."[51]

So, there were three issues to return on the normality. First was to complete the treaty, second to satisfy his colleagues about the "terms of trade" because the Prophet (ﷺ) accepted the conditions of the opponents. But we believe that the Prophet (ﷺ) had done it with the consent/guidance of Allah (SWT). The third issue was to abandon Umrah. Let us see these elements in detail.

The Treaty

It took place after exchange of ideas between the parties in many rounds of dialogue. According to Mubarikpuri,

When Quraish saw the firm determination of the Muslims to shed the last drop of blood for the defence of their Faith, they came to their senses and realized that Muhammad's followers could not be cowed down by these tactics. After some further interchange of messages, they agreed to conclude a treaty of reconciliation and peace with the Muslims. The clauses of the said treaty go as follows:

1. The Muslims shall return this time and come back next year, but they shall not stay in Makkah for more than three days.

2. They shall not come back armed but can bring with them swords only sheathed in scabbards and these shall be kept in bags.

3. War activities shall be suspended for ten years, during which both parties will live in full security, and neither will raise sword against the other.

4. If anyone from Quraish goes over to Muhammad without his guardian's permission, he should be sent back to Quraish, but should any of Muhammad's followers return to Quraish, he shall not be sent back.

5. Whosoever wishes to join Muhammad, or enter treaty with him, should have the liberty to do so; and likewise, whosoever wishes to join Quraish, or enter treaty with them, should be allowed to do so. The treaty was the first step towards normality It enabled Muslims to return peacefully to Madinah.

Satisfying colleagues

After a long discussion the parties arrived at a peace pact; nothing remained but to write an agreement. 'Umar jumped up and went to Abu. Bakr saying, 'Is he not God's apostle, and are we not Muslims, and are they not polytheists?' to which Abu Bakr agreed, and he went on: 'Then why should we agree to what is demeaning to our religion?' He replied, 'Stick to what he says, for I testify that he is God's apostle.' 'Umar said, 'And so do I' Then he went to the apostle and put the same questline to which the apostle answered, 'I am God's slave and His apostle. I will not go against His commandment, and He will not make me the loser.'[52] The statement clarifies the fact that the Prophet (ﷺ) had it done under the guidance of Allah SWT. It satisfied the companions because Allah's decree is the final and He holds the ultimate authority. And He knows what is good for us and what was better for the muslims at that time. The time showed the treaty was a success for the

Prophet (ﷺ) and his community because more people joined his hands during the pact and after two years Makkah fell to the hands of Muslims.

Abandoning Umrah

It was difficult for everyone to end Umrah, but Muslims must comply with the term of truce. Since the Prophet (ﷺ) was a role model so he started the end of Umrah himself. Lings describes the matter,

So, the Prophet (ﷺ) went to the camel which he himself had consecrated and sacrificed it, saying in a loud voice, so that the men could hear: *Bismi-Lliih, Allahu Akbar.* At these words the men leaped to their feet and raced to make their sacrifices, falling over each other in their eagerness to obey; and when the Prophet (ﷺ) called for Khirash - the man of Khuza'ah he had sent to Mecca before 'Uthman - to shave his head, many of the Companions set about shaving each other's heads so vigorously that Umm Salamah was afraid, as she afterwards remarked, that mortal wounds might be inflicted. But some of them merely cut locks of their hair, knowing that this was traditionally acceptable as a substitute. Meantime the Prophet (ﷺ) had retired to his tent with Khirash; and when the rite had been accomplished, he stood at the entrance with shaven scalp and said: "God have Mercy on the shavers of their heads!" Whereupon those who had cut their hair protested: "And on the cutters of their hair, O Messenger of God!" But the Prophet (ﷺ) repeated what he had said at first, and the voices were raised in protest still louder. Then after another repetition and a third thunderous protest he added: "And upon the cutters of their hair!" When asked afterwards why he had first prayed only for the shavers of their heads, he answered: "Because they doubted not."[53]

Slaughtering sacrificial animals, shaving head, and wearing normal cloths were the actions required to abandon umrah.

The Prophet (ﷺ) had done it himself and the companions followed him. Thus, the entire group attained normality i.e., they left for Madinah after performing required activities.

Recovery from the battle of Uhad

Muslims sustained extraordinary loss of human lives in this battle though they saved themselves from losing the battle. The Prophet (ﷺ) took a couple of measures to recover from the crisis. He planned the expedition prudently which gave muslims upper hand in the beginning of the event. Second, he turnaround from the caustic situation and collected his campanion at a single point. Third, he launched a counterattack on the enemy away from Madinah which helped him to recover physically and psychologically from the crisis. Let us examine these elements.

Plan of the battle

The Prophet (ﷺ) was an analytical thinker and a prudent planner. He had appointed his uncle Abbas (RA) to keep an eye on the enemy movement, plan, and programmes. Abbas (RA) sent a letter to the Prophet (ﷺ) well before the accumulation of Makken army to march towards the newly emerged state of Madinah about the programme of Quraysh.[54]

The Prophet (ﷺ) at once consulted migrants and Helpers because a war was on the brink of Madinah to define the plan of the battle. Everyone was ready to defend the sacred land; therefore, he appointed a small battalion to guard the Prophet (ﷺ). He also installed some troops at the entrances of the city to prevent any sudden attack.

In addition, the Prophet (ﷺ) had set up an information / intelligence team to keep an eye on the movement of the enemy. The team informed him in the first week of Shawal 6 AH that the enemy troops had encamped in the outstrips of the city. He called a high-level meeting of the consulting team or shoorah to discuss the defence strategy. Two opinions appeared: to remain in the city and defend it, the second was to fight in the open space. The Prophet (ﷺ) was in favour of the former while most of the young companions were supporting the later view. However, the Prophet (ﷺ) had selected the later view.[55]

The Prophet (ﷺ) had appointed his deputy for Madinah and organized the troops in three battalions: the migrants, Auws (The Helper tribe) and Khazrij (another Helper tribe). The Islamic army marched towards Uhud.[56]

Turning around

Muslims were winning the battle in the beginning as Mubarikpuri states,

War activities went on and on fiercely with the Muslims in full command of the whole military developments until the idolaters finally staggered and retreated, leaving all motives of alleged pride, and affected dignity in oblivion, and their standard trodden by the feet of the fighters with none ever courageous enough to approach it. It seemed as if the three thousand idolaters had been fighting thirty thousand Muslims and not merely several hundreds.

Ibn Ishaq said: "Then Allah sent down His Help unto the Muslims and verified His Promise to them. They chased the idolaters and evacuated them from their camp. No doubt it was a certain defeat." In a version by 'Abdullah bin Az-Zubair that his father had said: "By Allah, I was watching the servants of Hind bint 'Utbah and her women friends fleeing with their garments gathered up. No one was there to prevent us from capturing them.

In another version by Al-Barfi' bin 'Azib — mentioned in Sahih Al-Bukhari — he said: "When we fought them, they fled, and their women could be seen fleeing in the mountains with their anklets and legs revealed." The Muslims pursued the enemies putting them to sword and collecting the spoils.[57]

However, a flank attack from enemy while muslims were busy collecting spoils of war put them under heavy strain. The sudden attack confused them which made them scattered around the battlefield. But the Prophet (ﷺ) remained steadfast on his position and managed to gather his companions around him. The enemy wanted to harm him but a pragmatic strategy of the Prophet (ﷺ) with the help of Allah SWT enabled him to reorganise his army. Abu Sufyan visited the muslim camp and exchanged bitter words with Muslims. Ibn Ishaq reports his conversation.

When Abu Sufyan wanted to leave, he went to the top of the mountain and shouted saying, 'You have done a fine work; victory in war goes by turns. Today in exchange for the day (of Badr). Show your superiority, Bubal,' i.e., vindicate your religion. The apostle told 'Umar to get up and answer him and say, 'God is most high and most glorious. ", we are not equal. Our dead are in paradise; your dead in hell.' At this answer Abu Sufyan said to 'Umar, 'Come here to me.' The apostle told him to go and to see what he was up to. When he came Abu Sufyan said, 'I adjure thee by God, 'Umar, have we killed Muhammad?' 'By God, you have not, he is listening to what you are saying now,' he replied. He said, 'I regard you as more truthful and reliable than Ibn Qami'a,' referring to the latter's claim that he had killed Muhammad.

Then Abu Sufyan called out, 'There are some mutilated bodies among your dead. By God, it gives me no satisfaction, and no anger. I neither prohibited nor ordered mutilation,' 'when Abu

Sufyan and his companions went away, he called out, 'Your meeting-place is Badr next year.' The apostle told one of his companions to say, 'Yes, it is an appointment between us.'

Then the apostle sent 'Ali to follow the army and see what they were doing and what their intentions were. If they were leading their horses riding their camels. If they would be making for Mecca; but if they were riding the horses driving the camels, they would be making for Medina.

By God, said he if they make for Medina, I will go to them there. Then I will fight them.' 'Ali said that he followed their tracks and saw what they were doing. They were leading/loading their horses, riding their camels, and going towards Mecca.[58]

It suggests that muslims gathered themselves at a given point with the Prophet (ﷺ). Since the enemy stopped the battle therefore, muslims were getting afresh to have another round of the battle. However, if the enemy were to attack muslim families in Madinah then the Prophet (ﷺ) intended to defend them. Abu Sufyan was claiming a partial victory when he said you won in Badr, and we are winning here. But in Badr Quraysh took a flight towards Makkah and muslims claimed the spoils of war while muslims were there in the battlefield in Uhad. And Quraysh did not claim a blade of sword. So, it was an undecided encounter though muslims suffered more loss than the opponents. But loss does not mean a defeat. Thus, the Prophet (ﷺ) turned around the crisis with his viable plan.

Counterattack

Another real time action of the Prophet (ﷺ) put muslims on the driving seat. Since Quraysh and their allies marched to their hometown without finishing the job yet there was a chance of their return. The Prophet (ﷺ) realised it and decided to follow them to have another round of battle or forced the enemy to take its way to Makkah. Lings tells us the story of afresh move by the Prophet (ﷺ),

"The two Sa'ds of the Helpers and other leaders of Aws and Khazraj spent the night at the door of the Mosque and took it in turns to stand on guard, for there was still always the possibility that Quraysh might return; and early the next morning, when the prayer had been prayed, the Prophet (ﷺ) told Bilal to announce to them and to others that the enemy must be pursued. "But none shall go out with us," he said, "save those who were present at the battle of yesterday."

They made their first halt about eight miles from Medina. The enemy were by that time encamped at Rawha', which was not far ahead. On hearing this the Prophet (ﷺ) ordered his men to spread themselves over a wide area of ground and to gather as much wood as they could find, piling it up each man for himself in a separate pile. By sunset they had prepared over five hundred beacons, and when night had fallen every man set fire to his. The flames were seen everywhere, as if a great army were encamped there. This impression was confirmed for Abu Sufyan by a man of Khuza'ah who, though still an idolater, was friendly to the Muslims and who told him with deliberate untruth that the whole city of Medina had come out in pursuit of them, including all those who had stayed behind from Uhud and all their confederates. "By God," he said, "ye will not have moved off before ye have seen the forelocks of their cavalry." Some of Quraysh had wanted to return and attack Medina, but they now unanimously decided to press on with all speed for Mecca. None the less Abu Sufyan sent back a parting message for the Prophet (ﷺ) by some riders who were on their way to Medina for provisions. "Tell Muhammad from me," he said, "that we are resolved to come against him and his companions and to root them out, those that yet remain, from the face of the earth. Tell him this, and when ye reach 'Ukaz on your return I will load your camel with raisins." When they delivered the message to the Prophet (ﷺ), he answered in the words of a recent Revelation: God is our sufficiency, and supremely to be trusted is He,' He and his Companions spent the Monday, Tuesday and Wednesday at their camp, lighting beacons every night, and those were days of much needed rest and plenty. There had been an excellent fruit harvest the previous summer, and Sa'd ibn 'Ubadah had loaded thirty camels with dates, and others had been brought to be sacrificed. On the Thursday they returned to Medina.[59]

So, the Prophet (ﷺ) ensured any possibility of reattacking until he knew the enemy went to Makkah. Therefore, the crisis started with the invasion of Quraysh on Madinah ended with the journey of Muslim army to Hamra Al-Asad. It indicated that Muslims returned to normality. Christine and Mitroff has given two parameters for successful recovery.[60] Table 1 summarises the measures the Prophet (ﷺ) had taken to return to normality according to these standards.

Table 1   Key parameters/questions of recovery and measures of the Prophet (ﷺ)

Parameters/questions	Measures of the Prophet (ﷺ)
What are the minimal procedures and operations that we need to recover and conduct normal business?	1-The procedure was to accumulate the troops at a single point to show that Muslims army was in the battlefield. 2-The Prophet (ﷺ) also appointed a person to discourage enemy for

	reattacking Muslims. 3-The Prophet (ﷺ) launched a fresh military operation (March towards Hamra tul Asad) to follow the enemy. The Prophet (ﷺ) sent his intelligence people to know the activities of the opponents. They came to know that the enemy was preparing for returning to Makkah.
What are the key activities and tasks that we must perform to serve our most important customers?	Customer in this perspective are the muslims and their allies. They felt secure after the return of Quraysh to Makkah.

It implies people resumed their normal activities, but Muslims sustained human losses during the battle. It was the price of peace nations must undergo to live in tranquillity.

6 LEARNING

Introduction

"Learning, the last phase of crisis management, refers to adequate reflection and critical examination of the lessons learned from experiencing a crisis. Sadly, we have found that many organizations do not conduct this phase because of the false notion that an examination of past crises will "only reopen old wounds." Yet exactly the reverse has been found in those organizations that dedicate the time and resources to integrate lessons learned from their experiences back into their crisis management process. Well-prepared organizations examine the factors that enabled them to perform well, versus those that inhibited their performance. Furthermore, they do so without assigning blame (except in cases of malfeasance) so that all pertinent information--both positive and negative--can surface. Rather than searching for scapegoats, the emphasis should be on improving future capabilities and fixing current problems. We call this "no fault learning.""[61]

We have examined several episodes and the learning gained out of them during various events in the following pages.

The treaty of Hodhabia

Muslims learned a couple of lessons from the treaty of Hodhbia, the expedition of Hijrah and the conquest of Makkah.

Muslims learned at least *three points* from the treaty of Hodhabia. It is always helpful in a crisis to clarify the objectives of an event. Since war is not the ultimate solution of human problems yet it is beneficial to initiate peace process as soon as possible. War may last for a few days, week, or year but peace prevails for rest of the time. For instance, two world wars in recent history lasted for about five years each but people enjoyed peace after that. From 1945 to date the world is in a state of peace overall except a few instances. The war in Afghanistan lasted for twenty years but ended upon peace talks. The Vietnam war concluded on the victory of a party but there is peace in the country since then. One purpose of war is to establish peace. Therefore, initiating peace talks achieves the real objective of a war. The Prophet (ﷺ) had not only achieved it but advised for it. He said to the military leaders to the nearest effect that propose peace first and if the opponents do not accept it than initiate war. Look at this saying of the Prophet (ﷺ),

Narrated Sahl bin Sa`d: On the day of Khaibar, Allah's Messenger (ﷺ) said, "Tomorrow I will give this flag to a man through whose hands Allah will give us victory. He loves Allah and His Apostle, and he is loved by Allah and His Apostle." The people remained that night, wondering as to who would be given it. In the morning the people went to Allah's Messenger (ﷺ) and every one of them was hopeful to receive it (i.e., the flag). The Prophet (ﷺ) said, "Where is `Ali bin Abi Talib?" It was said, "He is suffering from eye trouble O Allah's Apostle." He said, "Send for him." `Ali was brought and Allah's Messenger (ﷺ) spat in his eye and invoked good upon him. So `Ali was cured as if he never had any trouble. Then the Prophet (ﷺ) gave him the flag. `Ali said "O Allah's Messenger (ﷺ)! I will fight with them till they become like us." Allah's Messenger (ﷺ) said, "Proceed and do not hurry. When you enter their territory, call them to embrace Islam and inform them of Allah's Rights which they should observe, for by Allah, even if a single man is led on the right path (of Islam) by Allah through you, then that will be better for you than the nice red camels.[62]

Thus, it is a clear instruction to be peaceful and the fight must be the last resort to establish peace. We have described three learning factors Muslims had learned out of the event

Clarification of his mission

It is important to clarify the mission of the organisation because it reduces misunderstanding and helps to resolve issues. We learn it from the ordeal of Hodhabia. The Prophet (ﷺ) and his companions encamped in Hodhabia, and Quraysh sent their envoy to inform him their attitude. Budayl, the ambassador said precisely that Quraysh would not allow Muslims to enter the holy city at any cost. "The Prophet (ﷺ) said: "We came not here for battle; we came only to make our pilgrimal rounds about the House. He that standeth in our way, him we shall fight; but I will grant them time, if they so desire it, to take their precautions and to leave the way clear for us." [63] It clarified the intent of the Prophet (ﷺ) and he put the ball in the court of Quraysh.

Initiating peace talks

It is always good but difficult to start dialogue. Since the objective of the Prophet (ﷺ) was not fight but peaceful performance of umrah, therefore, he sent Usman (RA) to Makkah for peace talks. It showed his action according to his intentions. When he received the rumour of his assignation, the Prophet (ﷺ) took oath or pledge of Rizwan. It united his team on a single objective and became ready to fight for the cause of Allah SWT. It also sent a message across the region that he had a right to enter Makkah as a pilgrim.

The talks eventually ended on a truce which avoided a fight and muslims found additional time to establish themselves. In addition, Allah SWT declared it as a "clear victory" And later events show that it was the prelude of the conquest of Makkah which put most of the Arabian Peninsula under the flag of Islam.

Avoided the mischievous of Quraysh.

While muslims were travelling on the way to Makkah, Quraysh tried to have a military encounter with them. But the Prophet (ﷺ) avoided it which enabled him to reach the suburb of Makkah. It increased threat to Quraysh which forced them to accept the offer of peace talks. Mubarikpuri describes the episode,

"The Quraishes, on their part, held a meeting during which they considered the whole situation and decided to resist the Prophet (ﷺ)'s mission at all costs. Two hundred horsemen led by Khalid bin Al-Waleed were despatched to take the Muslims by surprise during Zuhr (the afternoon) prayer. However, the rules of prayer of fear were revealed meanwhile and thus Khalid and his men missed the chance. The Muslims avoided marching on that way (The way of Khalid b Waleed) and decided to follow a rugged rocky one. Here, Khalid ran back to Quraish to brief them on the latest situation."[64] The Prophet (ﷺ) prevented an encounter to the band of Khalid because it was against the purpose of his mission, and he continued his journey.

The above discussion suggests that muslims learned that clarification of objectives, starting peace talks and avoiding any military engagement were key factors which made the crisis resolved. In connection with the peace talks, the Prophet (ﷺ) had suggested Quraysh to consider it before staring fight. He was the first to send his representative for the talks. Since his mission was doing Umrah peacefully yet he did not involve in any military campaign though the opponents wanted it.

The expedition of Hijrah

It was one of the major crises the Prophet (ﷺ) had encountered and managed. We can learn several lessons out of it: we have divided it into personal qualities and organisational matters.

Organisational matters

There is many learning aspects, but we have chosen two of them for this treatise to keep the discussion brief.

Planning

Since Hijrah was a successful journey yet it required planning. The author has examined it in an article which is enough to understand the phenomenon.[65] In addition, according to Ibn Ishaq

It was then that God gave permission to his Prophet (ﷺ) to migrate. Abu Bakr was a man of means, and at the time that he asked the apostle's permission to migrate, and he replied' Do not hurry; perhaps God will give you a companion, hoping that the apostle meant himself he (Abu Bakr (RA)) bought two camels .and kept them tied up in his house supplying them with fodder as part of preparation for departure … So, they hired 'Abdullah b. Arqat, whose mother was a woman of B. Sahm b. 'Amr, and a polytheist to lead them on the way, and they handed over to him their two camels and he kept them and *fed* them until the appointed day came.[66] So, Abu Bakr (RA) prepared the transport, and the Prophet (ﷺ) asked him to stay in Makkah whenever he wanted to migrate. The Prophet (ﷺ) asked Abu Bakr (RA) to stay behind to go with him and Abu Bakr (RA) prepared camels for the journey. Both actions are part of planning because planning means deciding in advance what to do. And decide on the resources needed for the plan.

Communication

Communication is a key enabler of decisions making and managing an organisation. It is evident from the Hijrah expedition that the Prophet (ﷺ) maintained constant communication with various companion especially Abu Bakr (RA) in this crisis. Ibn Ishaq reports,

A man whom I have no reason to doubt told me as from 'Urwa b. al Zubayr that 'A'isha said: The apostle used to *go* to Abu Bakr's house every day either in the early morning or at night; but on the day when he was given permission to migrate from Mecca he came to us at noon, an hour at Which he was not wont to come. As soon as he saw him Abu Bakr realized that something had happened to bring him at this hour. When he came in Abu Bakr gave up his seat to him. Only my sister Asma' and I were there, and the apostle asked him to send us away. 'But they are my two daughters, and they can do no harm, may my father and my mother be your ransom,' Said Abu Bakr 'God has given me permission to depart and migrate,' he answered. 'Together? -, asked Abu Bakr 'Together,' he replied. And by God before that day, I had never seen anyone weep for *joy*' as Abu Bakr wept then.[67]

In addition, we can learn a couple of other organisational issues such as project management, risk management and managing resistance to change' The author has dealt with these topics in a chapter length material elsewhere. Please see the reference for details. [68]

Personal qualities

We have included two instances from the life of the Prophet (ﷺ).

Extraordinary courage

The Prophet (ﷺ) had shown extraordinary courage when people reached the cave for his search. He said,

Narrated Abu Bakr: I was with the Prophet (ﷺ) in the Cave. When I raised my head, I saw the feet of the people. I said,

"O Allah's Messenger (ﷺ)! If some of them should look down, they will see us." The Prophet (ﷺ) said, "O Abu Bakr, be quiet! (For we are) two and Allah is the Third of us."⁶⁹ In the words of Lings, "The voices were now not far off - five or six men at least - and they were still approaching. The Prophet (ﷺ) looked at Abu Bakr, and said: Grieve not, for verily God is with us.! And then he said: "What thinkest thou of two when God is their third?" ⁷⁰ It suggests that a muslim manager must show bravery whenever it needed as the Prophet (ﷺ) had demonstrated it.

Saraqa was in search of the team of the Prophet (ﷺ) during the journey, he reached near the travellers and wanted to harm the Prophet (ﷺ), but Allah SWT saved him. Ibn Ishaq put it nicely,

(Saraqa says) I rode in pursuit of him, and my horse was going at a good pace he stumbled and threw me. I thought this was unusual, so I resorted to the divining arrows again and out came the detestable "Do him no harm." But I refused to be put off and rode on in pursuit. Again, my horse stumbled and threw me, and again I tried the arrows with the same result. I rode on, and at last as I saw the little band my horse stumbled with me, and its forelegs went into the ground, and I fell. Then as it got its legs out of the ground smoke arose like a sandstorm. When I saw that I knew that he was protected against me and would have the upper hand. I called to them saying who I was and asking them to wait for me' and that they need have no concern, for no harm would come to them from me. The apostle told Abu Bakr to ask what I wanted, and I said, "Write a document for me which will be a sign between you and me" and the apostle instructed Abu Bakr to do so.⁷¹

Accepting challenges (Adopted the way where robbers used to operate)

Similarly, the Prophet (ﷺ) came to know that there were two robbers on the way to Madinah. He decided to approach them and invited them towards Islam. Consequently, they embraced the true religion. People used to afraid of them, but the Prophet (ﷺ) showed courage to meet them for the sake of Islam. And Allah SWT made him successful in his purpose. Maulana Kandhelvi says about the occasion, "Rasulullaah (ﷺ) asked them their names, they said that they were called "Muhaanaan" ("The two contemptible ones"). Rasulullaah (ﷺ) said to them, "No. You two are 'Mukramaan' ('The two honoured ones')."[72]

Personal qualities are key for a leader to manage people and organisations. Courage is related with decision making; a brave manager takes risky decisions which can lead an organisation to exploit available opportunities such as taking new initiatives. For instances, the Prophet's (ﷺ) decision to adopt a dangerous way enabled two persons to enter in the fold of Islam. Since his mission was propagating Islam yet he managed to make it because of his decision.

The conquest of Makkah

Muslims learned couple of factors out of the campaign. The first of them was the secrecy i.e., to keep things in secrecy because it enabled waste of resources and ensures easy success. Secrecy of the intention of Muslims kept the loss of human lives minimum. If Quraysh were not attacking the battalion of Khalid b Waleed, there was no human loss during the expedition.

The Prophet (ﷺ) had made supplication for it, and he asked his companions to recover a letter the purpose of which was to inform Quraysh about the Prophet's (ﷺ) agenda.

Reflection/critical analysis

We have examined three instances about the learning. The purpose of learning is to investigate "the factors that enabled them to perform well and inhibited their performance". The factors that lead to the success of the campaign of Hodhabia was clarification of objective of the visit, initiation of peace talks and avoidance of military encounter. The factors that inhibit to achieve their aim was the conditions of the treaty. The Prophet (ﷺ) postponed the Umrah according to the stipulations of the treaty. The fundamental reason was the behaviour of Quraysh who stopped muslim for entering in the holy city.

During the expedition of hijrah, the Prophet (ﷺ) made bold decisions and remained steadfast in demanding situation. These were the key factors that enabled the Prophet (ﷺ) and his team to reach Madinah. The negative factor could impact the event was the action of Sarika who wanted to stop the team. But the Prophet (ﷺ) resolved it though the Divine help.

The Prophet (ﷺ) kept the event of conquest of Makkah secret to make it a success. The strength of the Muslim army and the strategy of the Prophet (ﷺ) to entertain Abu Sufyan were the positive factors that lead to the triumph. However, attack of a small band of Quraysh on the troops of Kahlid b Waleed (RA) was an attempt to make dents in the objectives of the Prophet (ﷺ) but they failed.

Improving future capabilities

The experience of the above events strengthened the capabilities of muslims. For instance, the treaty of Hodhbia enabled them to focus on the work of dawah. The Prophet (ﷺ) sent invitation letters to the kings and head of tribes etc to call them towards Islam. Many of them responded positively and the king of Abyssinia entered in the fold of Islam. The Prophet (ﷺ) performed Umrah the following year and Quraysh accepted him a key figure in the region of Hijaaz. Muslims captured Khyber after the treaty which enhanced their financial capabilities. The strength of muslim army was 1400 during the Hodhbia campaign but increased to 10,000 after about two years for the major event of Makkah.

The Hijrah expedition changed the landscape of Islamic moment. It changed the base camp which became a centre for the development of Islam as a leading religion in the Arabian peninsula and behind. Planning and effective communication were organisational level strength while decision making and managing odd situations came out as key characteristics of the Prophet (ﷺ).

The conquest of Makkah highlighted the importance of secrecy because it saved lives and muslims gained an easy victory. The incident of Khalid's (RA) troops did not overshadow the triumph of Islam.

7 CRISIS MANAGEMENT PLANNING

Introduction

Planning refers to deciding in advance about an issue, project, or process. The purpose is to prepare or prevent a crisis to happen. There were many crises the Prophet (ﷺ) had encountered and managed. Notable of them were seven major battles, the expedition of hijrah and the treaty of Hodhabia. The scale of threats in Makkah were individual level, the opponents were persecuting the Prophet (ﷺ) and his companions. Their objective was to stop them from preaching or practicing Islam. Nevertheless, the danger changed to an organisation level in Madinah because the target was the newly emerged muslims state. Therefore, many grave crises emerged. The Prophet (ﷺ) had defined a grand strategy to manage them. The grand strategy includes treaties with tribes living around Madinah and engagement of most powerful threat from Quraysh and their allies. Management of information about movements and activities of opponents irrespective of whosoever they were. We have examined them in the paragraphs to come.

Treaties with various tribes

Treaties with nearby tribes including Banu Khaza of Makkah under the treaty of Hodhabia and peace pacts with Jews and others were key initiative in this regard.

The Prophet (ﷺ) had made a treaty with the people of Madinah in Mina. The contents of the truce were,

1. To listen and obey in all sets of circumstances.
2. To spend in plenty as well as in scarcity.
3. To enjoin good and forbid evil.
4. In Allah's service, you will fear the censure of none.

5. To defend me in case I seek your help, and debar me from anything you debar yourself, your spouses, and children from. And if you observe those precepts, Paradise is in store for you.

In another version narrated by Ka'b, he said: The Prophet (ﷺ) began to speak, recited some Qur'anic verses, called people unto Allah, exhorted them to enter the fold of Islam and concluded saying: "I give you my pledge that you debar me from whatever you debar your women and children from." Here Albara' bin Ma'rur, caught him by hand, and said: "Oh yes, we swear by Allah, Who sent you as a Prophet (ﷺ) in Truth, that we will debar you from whatever we debar our women from. Have confidence in us, O Messenger of Allah. By Allah, we are genuine fighters and quite reliable in war, it is a trait passed down to us from our ancestors."[73]

When Quraysh knew it, they reacted furiously. Mubarikpuri describes it as,

No sooner did Quraish hear of this treaty than a kind of trouble provoking tumult began to mushroom in all directions. They realized quite fully that an allegiance of this sort is bound to produce far-reaching ramifications of direct impact on their lives and wealth. The following day, a large delegation comprising the leaders and arch-criminals of Makkah set out for the camp of the Madinese to protest severely against the treaty. They addressed the Madinese: "O people of Khazraj, it transpired to us that you have come here to conclude a treaty with this man (Muhammad) and evacuate him out of Makkah. By Allah, we do really hold in abhorrence any sort of fight between you and us." [74] Quraysh knew the potential impacts of the treaty which forced them for its opposition. The treaty was a plan for the future of Islam in Madinah. The history showed that the treaty was a corner stone in the spread of the religion in four corners of the world. It was a step for managing the current crisis of in search of an alternative place for the propagation of Islam. Ibn Ishaq argues about the journey of Ta'if, "In consequence of the growing hostility of Quraysh after Abu Talib's death the apostle went to Ta'if to seek help from Thaqif and their defence against his tribe ... The apostle sat with them and invited them to accept Islam and asked them to help him against his opponents at home."[75]

The treaty was a milestone in the life of the Prophet (ﷺ) because it was the basis of migration and propagation of Islam in Madinah.

Information Management

Information management is a key enabler of planning and managing crisis. It involves gathering, preserving and dissemination of relevant information on time. The author's book on the subject may be a source of Prophet's (ﷺ) strategy of information management.[76] However, a few episodes of the topic are here to make it short.

The Prophet (ﷺ) appointed Hazrat Abbass (RA) to keep an eye on the activities of Quraysh before the battle of Uhad.[77] The Prophet (ﷺ) had appointed a person from the tribe of Khaza whose Islam was unknown to Quraysh to find out the activities of Quraysh before the treaty of Hodhbia. He informed the Prophet (ﷺ) about the programme of the people of Makkah. They were determined to stop muslim form doing umrah.[78] The Prophet (ﷺ) received information of preparation of Ruman army from the Syrian traders prior to the expedition of Tabuk.[79]

Similarly, the Prophet (ﷺ) sent Ali (RA) to announce the dissolution of or completion of Memorandum of Understanding (MoUs). The Prophet (ﷺ) also dispatched many letters of invitation towards Islam to different kings or head of tribes etc. [80] It suggests that collation and dissemination of information was a regular activity of the Prophet (ﷺ). It helped him to plan various events and crises. For instance, when he received a letter from Abbas about the programme of Quraysh, he planned the response strategy to cope with the crisis of the battle of Uhad.

Planning for the battle of Trench

There were two phases of the planning: preventive measures and defining a defence plan for the battle of Trench.

Preventive measures

A battle is a crisis which happens suddenly but sometimes some events lead to it. Since two battles took place between Muslims and Quraysh yet they were expecting another battle because Quraysh wanted to take revenge. Therefore, the Prophet (ﷺ) continued its preparation through taking controlling/preventing measures. He sent a couple of army teams to manage emerging dangers which could turn into a significant crisis. It was also necessary to diminish the perception of Quraysh and their allies including those who were living around Madinah that Muslims were weak now due to heavy losses in Uhad. In fact, these measures were part of a grand plan to control present and potential crises that may emerge.

Mubarikpuri summarised the situation that arises after the battle of Uhad. He says,

Thus, we see that the Muslims turned into an attractive target of several potential dangers after they had lost their military credibility in the battle of Uhud. Muhammad, most wisely managed to hold all those hostile currents at bay, and even redeem the lost dignity of the Muslims and gain them anew fresh glory and noble standing. The first initiative he took in this process was Hamra' Al-Asad pursuit operation, whereby he could retain the Muslim military reputation. He succeeded in recovering his followers' dignity and awe-inspiring position in such a manner that astonished or even astounded both the Jews and hypocrites, alike, then he proceeded to crown his successful attempts by despatching military errands and missions. [81] He has described eight military expeditions including the "Second Badr". These were part of the plan to restrain the enemy Abu Salma (RA) campaign disabled Banu Asad of Khuzaimah and Abdullah bin Unees (RA) eliminated Khalid bin Sufyan Huzli. The Prophet (ﷺ) used to react in response to any emerging crisis; these two expeditions were part of it. However, the campaign of Bani Nazeer was a reactionary event. They were confederate of Muslims but has been conspiring against Islam. According to a well-known biographer

We have already spoken about the disgraceful behaviour of the Jews and how they were always thirsting to shed the blood of the Muslims and undermine the cause of Islam despite all the covenants and pledges they had given to the Prophet (ﷺ) Their behaviour fluctuated between resignation and slackness after the Banu Qainuqa' event and the murder of Ka'b bin Al-Ashraf, and rebellion coupled with treacherous clandestine contacts with Quraish and the hypocrites in order to establish an alliance against the Muslims after the battle of Uhud. Being inexperienced in war tactics, they resorted to conspiracy and intrigue hatching. They first declared open hatred and enmity and chose to play all sorts of tricks that might harm the Muslims but were incredibly careful not to initiate any sort of hostilities that might involve them in open war.

The Prophet (ﷺ) on his part, exercised the highest degree of patience with them but they went too far in their provocative deeds, especially after Ar-Raji' and Ma'una Well events; they even tried on his life.[82] Therefore, the Prophet (ﷺ) decided to settle the matter for ever. Consequently, the siege of Bani

Nazeer happened which ended on the expulsion the said people from their dwellings.

These events were the prelude of the battle of Trench. Abu Sufyan threatened muslims about another round of fight in Badr before their departure to Makkah following the battle of Uhad. The Prophet (ﷺ) accepted their challenge and travelled to the agreed place with his troops. Abu Sufyan also departed from Makkah with a strong military band. But when he knew the strength of Muslim army, therefore, abandoned the mission. But the Prophet (ﷺ) stayed at the specified place for a week or so. It implies the purpose was to fulfil the promise of the last year and to show that muslims were determined to defend at all costs.

Preparation of a trench

However, the real crisis appeared when the enemy gathered a huge army against Muslims and travelled to Madinah to eliminate them. Since the numerical strength of the enemy was far larger than the Muslim army yet the Prophet (ﷺ) used a unique technique for defence i.e., the digging of a trench which lied between the competing troops. Lings describes it briefly,

They (Quraysh) marched forth from Mecca-according to plan; and about the same time, with the connivance of 'Abbas, several horsemen from the Bani Khuza'ah set out with all speed for Medina to warn the Prophet (ﷺ) of the impending attack and to give him details of its strength. They reached him in four days, thus giving him only a week to prepare. He at once alerted the whole oasis and spoke words of encouragement to his followers, promising them the victory if only they would have patience, fear God, and obey orders. Then, as he had done at Uhud, he summoned them to a consultation at which many opinions were expressed as to what would be the best plan of action; but finally Salman rose to his feet and said: "O Messenger of God, in Persia when we feared an attack of horse, we would surround ourselves with a trench, so let us dig a trench about us now." Everyone agreed to this plan with enthusiasm.[83]

Planning for the battle of Uhad

The battle of Uhad was a one of the major crises muslims had ever encountered. Quraysh were furious for their first defeat in the battle of Badr and loss of key figures. They wanted to take revenge at any cost. Therefore, Quraysh mad preparations with extra ordinary enthusiasm to make things happen. Maulana Shibli and his colleague summed up the situation.

In Arabia a long series of wars could be started by the murder of a single man; and these wars could go on for hundreds of years. The defeated party considered revenge a sacred duty that could never be time-barred and had to be performed if the party was to maintain its existence. The battle of Badr had claimed a toll of seventy lives from the Quraish, most of them their top chiefs; and consequently, the whole of Mecca was thirsting for revenge. The original investment of the trade caravan which at the time of Badr had safely come back to Mecca had been returned to the shareholders but the profits had been kept in reserve.

When the mourning for the dead at Badr had toned down, the Quraish were reminded of their duty. A few leading personalities— Abu Jahl's son 'Ikrama being one of them, — persuaded those whose relations had been killed in the battle to accompany them to Abu Sufyan. They represented to him that Muhammad (peace and blessings of Allah be upon him) had dealt a death blow to their community and it was time to have a revenge. They wished to utilize for that purpose the profits in reserve. This was a request that was accepted before it was made. Now the Quraish had an idea of Muslim strength and knew that this time they would require much more than what they had at Badr. In Arabia the best way to excite people and work up feelings was to make use of poetic talent. The Quraish had two well-known poets, 'Amr Jumahi and Musafy. 'Amr Jumahi had been made a prisoner at Badr, but the Prophet (ﷺ) (peace and blessings of Allah be upon him) out of his clemency had set him free. Now at the request of the Quraish, 'Amr set out from Mecca acccmpanied by Musafy and they warmed up the tribes with their fiery tongues.

Women were another serviceable instrument to excite men and goad them to hold out to the last. With the tender sex in the rear, the Arab would put in a desperate effort to do or die, for in the event of defeat shame and dishonour would befall his women. Moreover, many a mother there was who had lost her offspring and was crying for vengeance. The bravest matrons had taken vows not to rest till they had sucked the blood of those who had slashed their sons to death. In short when the army was ready to move it was joined by ladies from respectable families.[84]

Planning strategy

When the Prophet (ﷺ) received the news of their march towards Madinah, he called an open consultation to define a defence plan. Lings put it nicely,

His first thought was not to go out from the city, but to stand a siege within its walls. He none the less wished to have his opinion confirmed by others, for it was by no means a conviction, so he held a consultation as to whether they should march out or not. Ibn Ubayy was the first to speak: "Our city," he said, "is a virgin that hath never been violated against us. Never: without severe losses have we gone out from her to attack an enemy; and none have entered her against us, but it is they who have suffered the losses. Therefore, let them be, O Messenger of God. Wretched will be their plight, so long as they stay; and when they return, they will return dejected and frustrated in purpose, with no good gained."

Many of the older Companions, of both the Emigrants and Helpers, inclined to the opinion of Ibn Ubayy. So, the Prophet (ﷺ) said: "Stay in Medina and put the women and children in the fortresses." Only when he had spoken thus did it become apparent that most of the younger men were burning with eagerness to march out against the enemy. "O Messenger of God," said one of them, "lead us forth against the enemy. Let them not think we fear them or that we are too weak for them." These words were met with a murmur of approval from various parts of the assembly, and others said much the same, with the added argument that their inactivity and their failure to take reprisal for their devastated crops would only serve to embolden Quraysh against them in the future, not to speak of the tribes of Najd. Harnzah and Sa'd ibn 'Ubadah and others of the more experienced now began to incline towards this view. "At Badr," said one of them, "thou hadst but three hundred men, and God gave thee mastery over them. And now we are many and have been hoping for this occasion and praying God for it, and He hath sent it to our very door."! Then one of the oldest men present roses to speak, a man of Aws named Khaythamah. He repeated many of the arguments already given against remaining on the defensive. Then he spoke on a more personal note. His son Sa'd was one of the few Muslims who had been slain at Badr. "Last night in my sleep," he said, "I saw my son. Most beautiful was his appearance, and I witnessed how it was given to him to fulfil his every wish amid the fruits and the rivers of the Garden. And he said: 'Come unto us and be our companion in Paradise. All that my Lord promised me to have I found to be true.' And I am old and I long to meet my Lord, so pray O messenger of God, that He will grant me martyrdom and the company of Sa'd in Paradise.

The Prophet (ﷺ) made a prayer for Khaythamah, no doubt a silent one, for the words are not recorded. Then another of the Helpers rose to speak, this time a man of Khazraj, Malik ibn Sinan. "0 Messenger of God," he said, "we have before us one of two good things: either God will grant us the mastery over them, and that is what we would have; or else God will grant us martyrdom. I care not which it may be, for verily there is good in both."

It was now clear, not only from the words that were spoken but from the general approval with which they were received, that the majority were against remaining behind the city walls.[85]

Thus, the Prophet (ﷺ) decided to step out of the city to meet the enemy in the open field. The plan was a pragmatic strategy which showed positive outcome for the muslims.

8 CASE STUDY: THE CRISIS MANAGEMENT IN THE BATTLE OF UHAD [86]

Introduction

The prophet (ﷺ) had employed many approaches for management of crises. The topic is concerned with management of sudden or unexpected events which could cause harm to an organisation. It creates threats for the management and impede the achievement of their objectives. Sometimes it challenges the existence of the organisation. It suggests that it must be managed to avoid its dysfunctional impacts on the reputation of the organisation and envisioned objectives.

The battle of Uhad characterised with several sudden or unexpected events. The prophet (ﷺ) had managed them successfully. It includes:

- The battle itself
- The action of hypocrites
- Change of designated position of archer's band
- Flank attack of the enemy

The purpose of the chapter is to analyse these events focusing on the crisis management strategy of prophet (ﷺ). To do it, we must find out the meaning of crisis and then needs to relate it with the events linked to the elements of crisis. However, it does not apply the crisis management framework of Christine and Mitroff because it was written independent of the framework.

What is crisis? [87]

The lingual definition of crisis is "a time of intense difficulty or danger." "a time when a difficult or important decision must be made." According to Collin dictionary "A crisis is a situation in which something or someone is affected by one or more very serious problems." In addition, "An unstable period, especially one of extreme trouble or danger in politics, economics, etc."⁸⁸ It suggests there are three key points in a crisis:

- Danger
- Difficulty
- Problem

Let me define them so that we can design a model to address the case study of Uhad.

Danger is defined as a <u>possibility that something harmful or unpleasant will happen</u>, or a person or thing that causes harm.⁸⁹ Difficulty means "the quality or state of being hard to do, deal with, or understand : the quality or state of being difficult"⁹⁰ Also a difficulty refers to <u>something that hinders you or causes you to have to face challenges</u>".⁹¹ Problem "is <u>something that has to be solved</u> or an unpleasant or undesirable condition that needs to be corrected."⁹² We can conclude out of the discussion that danger is the possibility that something harmful or unpleasant will happen, difficulty refers to something that hinders you or causes you to have to face challenges. And problem "is something that must be solved. Given that let us investigate the case study to find out what danger (s), difficulty, and problem the prophet (ﷺ) had encountered and managed.

The case in question

Let us analyse the case from the above perspective.

The danger is one of the three issues that are associated with crisis management. When the enemy forces were on the doorstep of the city, Mobarikpuri (1995) says that the danger was there that the enemy will invade Madhina. We understand from the definition of danger that it happens in the future. The arrival of the enemy was the eminent threat. Consequently, the prophet(ﷺ) had designed a strategy to manage it. The difficulty was the lack of resources compare to the opposition. If we compare the number of troops only; the ratio was 1:4. The Prophet (ﷺ) addressed the problem in the battlefield. The Prophet (ﷺ) had employed the smaller number of troops efficiently which enabled Muslim to gain victory in the first instance i.e., he appointed a band of archers at an entry point. If the band was defending the picket, the enemy did not dare to make a flank attack. When the band left the post, the enemy on flight reattacked. However, it increased the human loss of Muslims, but the enemy could not win the battle. Many writers declare it a defeat of Muslims, but many Muslim scholars concluded with compelling evidence that it was not a defeat.[93]

The infidels did not loot the spoils of war because the Muslim troops were there. The enemy left the battlefield rather than the Muslim army. The prophet (ﷺ) sent a band of seventy people to follow the enemy. The prophet(ﷺ) reinforced them with all the Muslim troops also in his command to Hamra Al-Asadh, a place eight miles towards Makkah.

There were other difficulties emerged during the campaign. The hypocrites left Muslim which was a fatal blow to Muslims who were already far less in numbers. But the prophet (ﷺ) had continued his journey. The courage and determination of Muslims did not derail them from the objective. The prophet (ﷺ) sent one of his companions to hypocrites to realise them their responsibility, but they were diehard in nature and wanted the defeat of Muslims. They had played the card of separation for the purpose. Mobarikpuri believes that well-articulated plan of the Prophet (ﷺ) overcome the deficiency of human resources.[94]

Another difficulty borne when the archers left their position. The men of the prophet (ﷺ) sustained losses but remained in the battlefield till the enemy lost the hopes of victory. Thus, the problem was addressed through additional sacrifice.

In addition, the martyrdom of Hamza (RA) reduced the combating power, but the army remained steadfast. Normally loss of a key figure changed the table in battles. But the inspirational leadership of the prophet (ﷺ) did not influence the problem.

In business terms when one of the products or market segment did not perform well then others sustained its weakness. It enabled the manager to continue the product or product line.

From the above discussion we can conclude that the prophet (ﷺ) had managed the key elements of crisis management i.e., danger, difficulty, and problems. We believe that it was achieved with the Devine Will and support. Allah helped his prophet (ﷺ) with His invisible hands.

The prophet (ﷺ) had managed numerous expeditions. The longest of them was the life in Makkah, Taif, migration to Abyssinia and Madinah. The Badr campaign etc. Uhadh added other aspects: the issue of hypocrites, the action of archers, the martyrdom of his uncle and his own injury to name a few. It strengthened his management skills and capabilities.

Crisis management

It "is the identification of threats to an organization and its stakeholders, and the methods used by the organization to deal with these threats."[95] Crisis management often requires decisions to be made within a short time frame, and *often after an event has already taken place*. To reduce uncertainty in the event of a crisis, organizations often create a crisis management plan.[96] It implies:

- Identification of threats
- Methods used to deal with them.
- Quick response is required after the incidence.
- Make a crisis management plan

Crisis: The battle

We take the model to analyse the crisis situations we have identified in the introduction.

The threat

According to Lings (1994)

"In Mecca the disaster of Qaradah intensified and quickened the preparations which had been in progress ever since Badr for an irresistible attack on Medina ... The moon reached its full, after which, a day or two later, came the anniversary of Badr; and in the last days of the month a sealed letter was brought to the Prophet (ﷺ) by a horseman who had ridden from Mecca to Medina in three days. It was from his uncle Abbas, warning him that an army of three thousand men was on the point of marching out against Medina. Seven hundred of the men were mailed, and there was a troop of horse two hundred strong. The camels were as many as the men, not counting the transport camels and those which carried howdahs for the women."[97]

Thus, the danger had emerged. When we look at the number of Quraysh troops and hardware, it was not difficult to estimate that the Makken army would crush four time less Muslim defendant. Remember that one year ago in Badr the ratio was 1:3; it is 1:4 now. The odds were significant.

Method of resolution

The Prophet (ﷺ) was expecting a severe response from Quraysh, but he kept an eye on them. He used to send small contingents to counter the caravans of Quraysh. The purpose was to realise them that the Prophet (ﷺ) was aware of them. And realised them that Madinah is a significant force residing on the trade routes. Lings put it as

The Meccans felt keenly the loss of their Red Sea caravan route. One of the disadvantages of the only alternative was that in the plain of Najd the wells were far apart. But now that the summer months were ending the journey could easily be managed by adding to the number of water-carrying camels; and they decided to send a rich caravan to Iraq consisting of bars of silver and silver vessels worth about a hundred thousand dirhems. It

was to be under the leadership of Safwan, Some of the Jews of Medina had secret information about the caravan and one of the Helpers happened to hear them discussing it. The Prophet (ﷺ) knew that Zayd had gifts of leadership, and he now sent him at the head of a hundred horse to waylay the caravan near Qaradah, which was one of the chief watering places along the route. The small and therefore more manageable force made it possible for Zayd to realise all the essentials of an effective ambush. Their sudden ferocious and unexpected onslaught put to flight Safwan and his fellows, while Zayd and his men returned to Medina in triumph, having become themselves the escort of all the Meccan transport camels with their rich loads of silver and other merchandise, and a few captives.[98]

It suggests that the Prophet (ﷺ) had a strategic plan for managing Quraysh and their confederates until they drink a bitter sip of complete defeat.

The plan

When the Prophet (ﷺ) received the letter from Abbas (RA) he had instructed the reader of the letter to keep the matter secret. The Prophet (ﷺ) had summand the meeting of leaders of both Migrants and Helpers or the "council of consultation." Two opinions emerged from the discussion: to remain in the city and to go out of the city to challenge the enemy. The Prophet's (ﷺ) opinion tilted towards the first option but the later was adopted after consultation.

Some other measures were taken to strengthen the plan. Saani (2019) summarised them in the following paragraph.[99]

A small battalion was appointed to guard the Prophet (ﷺ). Some troops were installed at the entrances of the city to encounter any sudden attack.[100] All people living outside Madinah were brought in with their animals.[101] Patrolling teams were set up to keep an eye on the movement of the enemy.

In addition, the Prophet (ﷺ) had also set up an information / intelligence team to keep an eye on the movement of the enemy...

He led the Jummah prayer, motivated people for the battle and announced that everyone should get prepared for it. People were happy, and they gathered at the time of Asr salah. The Awali team had also arrived; meanwhile the Prophet (ﷺ) dressed himself for the combat.

It suggests that security measures were taken to ensure safety of the people due to any sudden attack by the enemy. A plan of action was made to encounter the opponents. The human resources were consolidated for a possible armed encounter. Although there was a scarcity of supplies yet whatever was available was collected and placed in the custody for use.

The result

There are many views about the outcome of the endeavour. Mobarikpuri (1995) writes,

War activities went on and on fiercely with the Muslims in full command of the whole military developments until the idolaters finally staggered and retreated, leaving all motives of alleged pride, and affected dignity in oblivion, and their standard trodden by the feet of the fighters with none ever courageous enough to approach it. It seemed as if the three thousand idolaters had been fighting thirty thousand Muslims and not merely several hundreds.

Ibn Ishaq said: "Then Allâh sent down His Help unto the Muslims and verified His Promise to them. They chased the idolaters and evacuated them from their camp. No doubt it was a certain defeat." In a version by 'Abdullah bin Az-Zubair that his father had said: "By Allâh, I was watching the servants of Hind bint 'Utbah and her women friends fleeing with their garments gathered up. No one was there to prevent us from capturing them."[Ibn Hisham 2/77]

In another version by Al-Barâ' bin 'Azib — mentioned in Sahih Al-Bukhâri — he said: "When we fought them, they fled, and their women could be seen fleeing in the mountains with their anklets and legs revealed."[Sahih Al-Bukhari 2/579] The Muslims pursued the enemies putting them to sword and collecting the spoils.[102]

Siddiqi beautifully describes the movement of truth, at last the idolaters perceived that safety was in "flight" only. Even their women inspirers ran away. The Muslims started to collect booty for which they deserved.

However, the situation changed when an archer squad left their appointed position. Enemy was keenly observing the situation; they fund a gap and took the opportunity to initiate a flunk attack. The Muslims were not ready for it were perceiving that the battle was over. The infidels caused a lot of loss to the Muslim ranks but could not made a decisive attack. Nevertheless, the Muslims got together around the Prophet (ﷺ) and made a defensive move. The enemy tried to break the human wall erected around the centre of Islam, but their efforts did not work. They lost the hopes of victory and left the battlefield.

Siddiqi (1997) concludes the discussion, the Muslims sustained loss due to a blunder, but they were neither defeated nor their power weakened. Therefore, the Prophet (ﷺ) had sent a battalion of seventy troops to follow the Makken army. The Prophet (ﷺ) himself was behind them up to Hamra-Alasadh, a place eight miles away from Madinah. The infidels realised their blunder i.e., they did not cash the upper hand they had in the later part of the battle.

9 CONCLUSIONS

The significance of Crisis Management (CM)

According to Mitroff crisis management "is a series of ongoing, interrelated assessments or audits of kinds of crises and forces that can pose a major threat to a company's main products, services, ... employees, environment, and communities." [103] It implies it was related with an organisation (Business, service or governmental etc.) at small scale, but the Prophet (ﷺ) had applied it at large scale i.e., state level. The frequency of natural disasters in the recent years especially the tsunami of 2004 which effected many countries and consumed thousands of lives necessitated to considered crisis management seriously. Fiscal crisis of 2007-2008 influenced the world economy where many countries lost their resources. Similarly, the cost-of-living crisis in the UK and elsewhere due to the European war demanded heads of states and even group of countries like European Union (EU) to manage the crisis. Thus, the importance of the subject increased many folds as compared to recent past. Although the book is not the response of these circumstances, yet it befits the situation that is coincident. The original purpose of the book was to expand the boundaries of Islamic Management Theory upon which the author has been working since a decade or so.

Common factors

"Key insights from the crisis management literature could be summarized as follows: crises are _commonplace_ (Wisenblit, 1989); _crises evolve in phases_ (Pearson and Clair, 1998); companies with specific _crisis management plans_ and adequate resources are likely to face lower damages when faced with a crisis (Cloudman and Hallahan, 2006; Penrose, 2000); and _effective communication strategies_ are extremely important for containing the damage because of a crisis

(Berge, 1990)." [104] Let us see what was in the crisis management strategy of the Prophet (ﷺ).

Crises are commonplace.

The life of the Prophet (ﷺ) was full of crisis. He had to lead/sent 82 military expeditions in 8 years.[105] In addition, hijrah to Madina and two such events to Abyssinia also happened. It implies every month he fought a battle or sent a military scout to manage enemies of Islam. When he used to receive information about some emerging crisis from a tribe/area, he used to settle it politically through making peace truce. However, from crisis management perspective it was a crisis, therefore, it was necessary to manage it. There were scores of such events which he had managed. It implies crisis was common during his life span.

Evolve in phases.

Some events or a series of events take time to become a crisis. For instance, the hijrah of the Prophet (ﷺ) was the result of several events that took place in Makkah. Persecution of Quraysh, the martyrdom of Summaya (RA), tortures of Bilal and Khubab were some instances that lead the hijrah. Notable of the events was the emergence of Islam in Madinah; the truce of Uqbaas in Mina and invitation of Ansaar. The final nail in the coffin was the plan of Quraysh to assassinate the Prophet. (ﷺ) In other words, these events were the reasons of the crisis of Hijrah i.e., the Prophet (ﷺ) had managed the crisis of his safety in Makkah though hijrah.

Management plans and effective communication

Management of crisis implies defining long term plans to tackle crisis. We have discussed the matter in detail in chapter seven. The Prophet (ﷺ) had made plans for managing individual battles and political situations. The author has discussed the Prophet's (ﷺ) planning strategy elsewhere. Interested reader can consult the sources (Please see other books by the author below).

The communication strategy was also part of chapter seven above. Specific examples of communication strategy are in the individual instances of crisis such a s various battles, hijrah and the treaty of Hodhbia.[106]

Concluding remarks

According to Mitroff "Some crises are inevitable no matter how well prepared an organization is. Both as a field of research and as a corporate function, Crisis Management (CM) is still new, and as a result it is neither well understood nor widely accepted. This is not to say that more advanced and developed CM programs could prevent all organizational crises from occurring. Indeed, complete prevention is not necessarily the goal of CM. However, there is evidence that effective CM would allow organizations to recover much faster and learn from major crises more effectively."[107] Nitin concludes that "organizations with a strong commitment to doing the right thing for stakeholders and a high readiness are most likely to effectively respond to crises. Organizations lacking in one of the two critical dimensions (commitment to stakeholders and/or readiness), on the other hand, are likely to have ineffective responses with possible post-crisis losses." [108]

His crisis response was sometimes immediate (e.g., the Bait-e-Rizwaan) and other times with some delay (e.g., the incident of Bair-e-Maunah).

BIBLIOGRAPHY

Adair, John (2010) The Leadership of Muhammad (ﷺ), New Delhi: Kogan Page India Private Limited.

Al-Bahaqi, Abi Bakker Ahmad Al-Hussain (2009) Dhalail Al-Nabuwwa, Karachi: Dharul Ishaat.

Alnoor Holdings Group (2011) The Prophet (ﷺ) of Islam MUHAMMAD, Biography & Practical Guide to the Moral Bases of the Islamic Civilization, Alnoor Holdings Group Qatar.

Allen, Louis A. (1958) Management and organization, New York: McGraw-Hill.

Al-Qahtani, Saeed bin Ali bin Wahf (2007) A Mercy to the Universe, Riyad: Maktaba-Darussalam.

Behaqi, Abi Baker Ahmad bin Hussain (2009) Dhalail Al-Nabuwwa (Translated in Urdu by Maulana Muhammad Ismael Al-Jarwi); Karachi: Dharul Ishaat.

Chesbrough, H. W. "The era of open innovation." MIT Sloan Management Review 44, no. 3 (2003a): 35-41.

Chesbrough, H. W. Open Innovation: The New Imperative for Creating and Profiting from Technology. (Boston: Harvard Business Press, 2003b)

Chesbrough, H. W. 2006. "The era of open innovation." In Managing Innovation and Change, edited by David Moyle, 127-138. London: Sage Publications Ltd.

DeCenzo, David A. and Stephen P. Robbins (2010) Human Resource Management, New York: John Wiley & Sons.

Dess, Gregory G., G. T. Lumpkin, Alan B. Eisner (2006) Strategic Management: Text and Cases, New York: Irwin/McGraw-Hill.

Dyck, B and Mitchell J Neubert (2009) Principal of Management, South-Western.

Fulop, L, and S Linstead (1999) Management, A critical text, London: Macmillan.

Gilani, Mnazar Ahsan Gilani (1936) Al-Nabi Al-Khatam Sallallaho Alaihay Wasallam (Urdu), Jayyad Barqi Press: Dehli.

Haimann, Theo and Raymond L. Hilgert (1972) Supervision: Concepts and Practices of Management, South-Western Publishing Company.

Hameed Ullah, M. (2006) The Prophet's (ﷺ) Establishing a State and his Succession, Beacon Books: Lahore.

Haykal, Muhammad Husayn, Translated by Isma'il Razi A. al-Faruqi, The Life of Muhammad (ﷺ)http://www.witness-pioneer.org/vil/Books/MH_LM/default.htm

Ibn Ishaq Sirat Rasoul Allah (SWT), An abridged version, https://ia800206.us.archive.org/12/items/Sirat-lifeOfMuhammad By-ibnIshaq/SiratIbnIahaqInEnglish.pdf

Ibn Kathir, (2006) The Life of the Prophet (ﷺ) Muhammad, V. 1, Reading: Garner Publishing Limited. Copyright 1998 The Centre for Muslim Contribution to Civilization.

Iqbal, Javed, and Muhammad Mushtaq Ahmad (2009) Planning in the Islamic Tradition: The Case of Hijrah Expedition, INSIGHTS 01(3), 37-68.

Kaandhlawi, Muhammad Zakarya (1997), Fazail-e-Hajj, Lahore: Kutibkhana Faizi.

Kaandhlawi, Muhammad Yusaf (2012), Hayatus Sahabah, Delhi: Islamic Books Services.

Kaandhlawi, Muhammad Zakarya (1997), Fazail-e-Amaal, Lahore: Kutibkhana Faizi.

Koontz, Harold, and Heinz Weihrich (2006) Essentials of Management, New Delhi: Tata McGraw-Hill Education, pp. 81-84.

Kreitner, R (2009) Principal of Management, South-Western.

Lings, M (1994) Muhammad, his life based on the earliest sources, Lahore: Suhail Academy.

Mansoorpuri, Muhammad Salman Sulaiman, Rahma-tul-Alameen, Lahore: Maktaba Rahmania.

Mayo, E. (1933), The Human Problems of an Industrial Organization, McMillan, New York, NY.

Mubarakpuri, Safiur Rahman (1995) "The Sealed Nectar" (Ar-Raheeq Al-Makhtum), Lahore: Al-Maktba Alsalfia.

Muhammad ibn Ishaq, (2004) The Life of Muhammad, Oxford University Press, Karachi.

Nadvi, Sulaiman Hussaini (2005) Khutbat-e-Seerat, Karachi: Zam-Zam Publishers.

Noamani, Shibli and Syed Solaiman Nadhvi (2004) Seeratun-Nabi, Karachi: Dharul-Ishaat.

Pea, Roy D. (2015) What Is Planning Development the Development of? Accessed: April 2015, http://web.stanford.edu/~roypea/RoyPDF%20folder/A11_Pea_82d.pdf

Peter H. Langford, Cameron B. Dougall, Louise P. Parkes, (2017) "Measuring leader behaviour: evidence for a "big five" model of leadership", Leadership & Organization Development Journal, Vol. 38 Issue: 1, pp.126-144, https://doi.org/10.1108/LODJ-05-2015-0103

Phalwari, Muhammad Jaafer (1995) Peghambr-e-Insaniat, Lahore: Idara Sakafat-e-Islamia.

Razi, Muhammad Wali (1987) Hadhi-e-Alam, Dharul-Ilm: Karachi.

Robbins, Stephen, and Mary Coulter (2017) Management, New Delhi: Pearson Education.

Saani, Javed Iqbal (2017) Prophet Muhammad (ﷺ) as a planning expert, London: Intellectual Capital Enterprise Limited.

Saani, Javed Iqbal (2016) Responsibilities of Managers: Selected Ahadith, available on amazon.co.uk. (Paperback edition)

Schumpeter, J. A. (1934). *Theory of Economic Development*. Cambridge, MA: Harvard University Press.

Shoqi, Abu Khalil (2002) Atlas-Seerat-e-Nabvi, Darussalam: Lahore.

Siddiqi, Naeem (1997) The Benefactor of Humanity (Mohsin-e-Insaniyat), Dehli: Markazi Matabah Islami Publishers.

Smith, Mike (2007) Fundamentals of Management, Berkshire: McGraw Hill Education.

Stogdill, R.M. (1957), Leader Behaviour: Its Description and Measurement, Bureau of Business Research, College of Commerce and Administration, Ohio State University, Columbus.

Time Management Guide (2015) What is planning and why you need to plan, Accessed: April 2015, http://www.time-management-guide.com/planning.html

Books of Ahadith

Imam Muhammad ibn Isma`il al-Bukhari al-Ju`fi (1983) Sahih Al-Bukhari, Translated by Muhammad Muhsin Khan, Lahore: Kazi Publications.

Imam Muhammad ibn Isma`il al-Bukhari al-Ju`fi (1983) Al-Adab al-Mufrad, www.darsusalam.com

Imâm Abut Hussain Muslim bin al-Hajjaj, SahIh Muslim, Translated by Nasiruddin al-Khattab, Riyadh, 2007, Maktaba Dar-us-Salam.

Imam Muslim ibn al-Ḥajjāj al-Qushayrī (1971-75) Translated by Abdul Hameed Siddiqui Sahih Muslim, Lahore, Sh. Muhammad Ashraf.

Imâm Hâfiz Abu Dawud, Sunan Abu Dawud Sulaiman bin Ash'ath, Maktaba Dar-us-Salam, Riyadh, 2007.

Imäm Hãfiz Abü 'Elsa Mohammad Ibn 'Elsa At-Tirmidhi, Jamia' At-Tirm1dhi, English Translation by Abu Khaliyl, Riyadh, 2007, Maktaba Dar-us-Salam.

Imiim Hiifiz Abu Abdur Rahmiin Ahmad bin Shu'aib bin 'Ali An-Nasa'i, Sunan An-Nasa'i, Riyadh, 2007, Maktaba Dar-us-Salam.

Imam Muhammad Bin Yazeed ibn Majah Al-Qazwinf, Sunan Ibn Majah Translated by Nasiruddin al-Khattab, Riyadh, 2007, Maktaba Dar-us-Salam.

Abu Zakaria Al-Nawawi, Riyad-us-Saliheen, Riyadh, 2007, Maktaba Dar-us-Salam.

Imam Malik bin Ans (رضي الله عنه), Muwatta Imam Malik, translated in Urdu by Allama Molana Abdul Hakeem Akhtar Shahjahanpuri, Lahore: Fareed Book Stall, accessed on 14 November 2017, https://readingpk.com/muwatta-imam-malik-imam-muhammad-malik/ https://www.sunnah.com

INDEX

A

Abbass (RA), 42

Abdurrehman Bin Ouff (RA), 42

Abu Bakr (RA), 42

Abu Hurairah, Ix, Xi

Aggressive Behaviour, 53

Ali (RA), 42, 103, 108

Allah (SWT), Ix, X, Xi, Xii, Xvii, Xix, Xx, 42, 46, 47, 48, 104

Allegiance, 80

Apostle, 52, 58, 62, 63, 72, 73, 74, 81

Appointed, 60

Arab, 40, 41, 42

Asim Bin Addi (RA), 42

Assessments, 100

Audits, 100

B

Battle, 40

Behaviour, 106

Boundaries, 100

Byzantine, 41

C

Campaign, 41, 42

Case Study, 119

Change, 119

Charity, Xiii

Communication, V, 47, 73, 77, 100, 101, 102

Community, 34, 59, 85

Companions, 42, 45, 46, 47

Conquest Of Makkah, Iv, 51, 68, 70, 75, 76, 77

Consultation, 38, 44, 47, 84, 86, 95

Contemporary, Xx

Contingency Theory, 25

Contributors, 42

Crisis, Iii, Xx, 24, 25, 26, 29, 34, 36, 37, 38, 45, 50, 56, 60, 63, 65, 68, 71, 73, 79, 80, 81, 82, 83, 84, 90, 91, 93, 94, 100, 101, 102, 122

Crisis Management Model, Iii, 26

Crisis Management Perspective, 101

D

Damage Containment, 26, 50

Danger, 24

Day Of Judgement, X

Dean Faculty Of Management Sciences, Vii

Defensive Measures, 33

Deputy, 46

Difficulty, 24, 91

Divine, 29, 45, 76

E

Empire, 41

Enthusiasm, 85

Environment, 50, 100

European, Vii, 100

Event, Iv, 25, 29, 33, 38, 39, 40, 45, 50, 51, 60, 68, 70, 76, 77, 83, 86, 93

Expedition, 42

F

Flank Attack, 50, 62, 92

Forgiveness, X

Framework, 36, 90

G

God, Ix

Government, Vii

H

Hadith, Ix, X, Xi, Xii, Xiii

Hajj, *105*, 121

Hamra-Al-Asad, 51

Hazard, 26, 122

Hodhabia, 45, 46, 116

Hypocrites, 41

I

Ibn Ishaq, 104

Information, Xvii, 60

International Islamic University Islamabad, Vii, Xvii

Investment, 85

IQRA University Islamabad, Vii

Islam, 47, *103*

Islamic, Vii, X, Xvii, 103, 105

Islamic Management Theory, 115

J

Jami` At-Tirmidhi, Xi

Javed Iqbal, I, Ii, Vii, Xx, 106

Jeopardy, 26, 122

Journey, 42

K

Kaaba, 47

Ka'bah, 45

Khaza, 46, 47

Knowledge, Ix

L

Leader, Xi, 106

Leadership, Xx, 33, 43, 93, 95, 106

Learning, Ix, 26, 68, 70, 72, 76

Lings, 43, 45, 105

M

Madinah, 40, 41, 42, 44, 46, 60

Makkah, 42, 46, 47

Management, 107

Managerial Implications, 115

Manpower, 42

Mecca, 45

Medina, 42

Message, Xx, 36, 38, 46, 47, 53, 64, 70

Messenger of Allah (SWT) (ﷺ), Ix, Xi, Xiii

Migrants, 60

Milestone, 29, 81

Military, 116

Military Expeditions, 83, 101

Mission, Iv, 45, 46, 70, 71, 75, 84

Mitroff, 26, 50, 65, 90, 100, 102

Mosque, Xii

Mota, 40

Motivation, 117

Mu'adh, Xiii

Mubarikpuri, 41

Muhammad Bin Musalmah (RA), 42

Muntakhib, X

Muslim, 40, 41

Muslims, 40, 41, 42, 45, 46, 47, 48

Mutilation, 62

Muwatta Malik, Xiii

N

Namus, 29

Negotiation, 56, 57

Numerical Strength, 84

P

Paradise, Xi

Participants, 42

Peace, Iv, 30, 46, 47, 57, 58, 66, 68, 70, 71, 76, 79, 85, 101

Performance, Vii, 68, 70, 76

Peril, 27, 122

Personal Qualities, Iv, 73, 75

Pilgrimage, 45

Plan, V, 30, 31, 33, 39, 40, 43, 51, 60, 63, 72, 80, 82, 83, 84, 86, 88, 92, 93, 95, 96, 101, 107

Planning, V, Xx, 72, 77, 79, 82, 85, 86, 105, 106, 118

Pledge of Rizwan, 70

Polytheists, 58

Potential Threat, 33

Prayers, Xv, Xix

Preventing Measures, 82

Probing And Prevention, 26

Problem, 24, 91, 115

Process, 56, 57, 68, 79, 82

Project, Xvii, 73, 79

Prophet (ﷺ), Xi, Xx, 40, 41, 42, 43, 103

Proposals, 46

Provocative Deeds, 83

Q

Qualities Of Good Leader, Ix, X

Quraysh, 45, 46, 47

R

Rasulullah, X

Rawalakot, Vii

Readiness, 102

Recovery, 26, 56, 65

Reflection, 68

Regaining, 56

Research, Vii, 102

Resources, 42

Responsibilities Of Managers, 118

Risk Factors, 26, 36

Risk Management, 73

Riyad As-Salihin, *Xiii*

Romans, 40, 41

S

Saad Bin Ubaidhah (RA), 42

Sahabah, 105

Sahih Muslim, 107

Sakeef, 30

Salat, Xi, Xiii

Salman Al-Farisi, 44

Serviceable Instrument, 86

Siddiqi, 37, 97, 107

Signal Detection, 26

Simulation Exercises, 36

Stakeholders, 25, 29, 93, 102

Strategic Thinker, 60

Strategy, 44, 61

Subordinates, X

Sustain the Damage, 50

T

Talha (RA), 42

Team, 60

Threats, 24, 25, 79, 90, 93

Trench, 44

Tribes, V, 32, 33, 34, 37, 38, 40, 41, 42, 43, 46, 47, 77, 79, 81, 86, 87

Troops, 60

U

Umer (RA), 42

Umm Salamah (RA), 45

Umrah, 46, 47

University Of Hull., Vii

Usman (RA), 42, 47

W

Warning Signs, Iii, 26, 29

Worship, Ix

Z

Zulhalifah, 46

OTHER BOOKS BY THE AUTHOR (S)

Extension of Islamic Management Style

1. Prof Dr. Javed Iqbal Saani (2022) **Islamic Business Case Studies**, Intellectual Capital Enterprise Limited, London, available on Amazon (Paperback edition)
2. Prof Dr. Javed Iqbal Saani (2022) **Allah's Decision: He is the best to decide**, Intellectual Capital Enterprise Limited, London, available on Amazon (Paperback edition)
3. Prof Dr. Javed Iqbal Saani (2022) **Managing Resistance to Change: The Approach of the Prophet (ﷺ)**, Intellectual Capital Enterprise Limited, London, available on Amazon (Paperback edition)
4. Prof Dr. Javed Iqbal Saani (2022) **Islamic Perspective of Entrepreneurship**, Intellectual Capital Enterprise Limited, London, available on Amazon (Paperback edition)
5. Prof Dr. Javed Iqbal Saani (2021) **Learning of Managerial Ideas from Quran**, Intellectual Capital Enterprise Limited, London, available on Amazon (Paperback edition)
6. Prof Dr. Javed Iqbal Saani (2021) **Islamic Guidelines for Administrators**, Intellectual Capital Enterprise Limited, London, available on Amazon (Paperback edition)
7. Prof Dr. Javed Iqbal Saani (2020) **Principles of Islamic Management**, Intellectual Capital Enterprise Limited, London, available on Amazon (Paperback edition)

Discovery of Islamic Management Theory

8. Prof Dr. Javed Iqbal Saani (2020) **Introduction to Islamic Management Theory**, Intellectual Capital Enterprise Limited, London, available on Amazon (Paperback edition)
9. Prof Dr. Javed Iqbal Saani (2021) **How I have Discovered Islamic Management Theory?** Intellectual Capital Enterprise Limited, London, available on Amazon (Paperback edition)

Investigations of related topics

10. Prof Dr. Javed Iqbal Saani (2021) **The Concept of Reward in Islamic Management Theory**, Intellectual Capital Enterprise Limited, London, available on Amazon (Paperback edition)
11. Prof Dr. Javed Iqbal Saani (2021) **The Value of Work in Islamic Management Theory**, Intellectual Capital Enterprise Limited, London, available on Amazon (Paperback edition)
12. Prof Dr. Javed Iqbal Saani (2020) **Decisions Making Approach of the Prophet [PBUH]**, Intellectual Capital Enterprise Limited, London, available on Amazon (Paperback edition)
13. Prof Dr. Javed Iqbal Saani (2020) **Problem Solving Approach of the Prophet [PBUH]**, Intellectual Capital Enterprise Limited, London, available on Amazon (Paperback edition)
14. Prof Dr. Javed Iqbal Saani (2020) **Prophet (ﷺ) Muhammad's [PBUH] Selection of Team Leaders**, Intellectual Capital Enterprise Limited, London, available on Amazon (Paperback edition)
15. Prof Dr. Javed Iqbal Saani (2020) **Key Managerial Decisions of the Prophet (ﷺ) [PBUH]**, Intellectual Capital Enterprise Limited, London, available on Amazon (Paperback edition)
16. Prof Dr. Javed Iqbal Saani (2020) **Prophet (ﷺ) Muhammad [PBUH] & Evolution of Management Theory**, Intellectual Capital Enterprise Limited, London, available on Amazon (Paperback edition)

Finding of Managerial Implications of Major Expeditions & Ideas

17. Prof Dr. Javed Iqbal Saani (2020) **Managerial Implications of Five Pillars of Islam**, Intellectual Capital Enterprise Limited, London, available on Amazon (Paperback edition)
18. Prof Dr. Javed Iqbal Saani (2020) **Managerial Implications of the Conquest of Khyber**, Intellectual

Capital Enterprise Limited, London, available on Amazon (Paperback edition)
19. Prof Dr. Javed Iqbal Saani (2019) **Managerial Implications of the Major Expeditions of the Prophet (ﷺ) [PBUH]**, Intellectual Capital Enterprise Limited, London, available on Amazon (Paperback edition)
20. Prof Dr. Javed Iqbal Saani (2019) **Managerial Implications of the Major Military Expeditions of the Prophet (ﷺ) [PBUH]**, Intellectual Capital Enterprise Limited, London, available on Amazon (Paperback edition)
21. Prof Dr. Javed Iqbal Saani (2019) **Managerial Implications of the Major Non-Military Expeditions of the Prophet (ﷺ) [PBUH]**, Intellectual Capital Enterprise Limited, London, available on Amazon (Paperback edition)
22. Prof Dr. Javed Iqbal Saani (2019) **Managerial Implications of the Treaty of Hodhabia**, Intellectual Capital Enterprise Limited, London, available on Amazon (Paperback edition)
23. Prof Dr. Javed Iqbal Saani (2019) **Managerial Implications of the Battle of Trench**, Intellectual Capital Enterprise Limited, London, available on Amazon (Paperback edition)
24. Prof Dr. Javed Iqbal Saani (2019) **Managerial Implications of the Conquest of Makkah**, Intellectual Capital Enterprise Limited, London, available on Amazon (Paperback edition)
25. Prof Dr. Javed Iqbal Saani (2019) **Managerial Implications of the Battle of Hunain**, Intellectual Capital Enterprise Limited, London, available on Amazon (Paperback edition)
26. Prof Dr. Javed Iqbal Saani (2019) **Managerial Implications of the Battle of Uhadh Campaign**, Intellectual Capital Enterprise Limited, London, available on Amazon (Paperback edition)
27. Prof Dr. Javed Iqbal Saani (2019) **Managerial Implications of the Tabuk Campaign**, Intellectual Capital Enterprise Limited, London, available on Amazon (Paperback edition)

28. Prof Dr. Javed Iqbal Saani (2018) **Managerial Implications of the Hijrah Expedition**, Intellectual Capital Enterprise Limited, London, available on Amazon (Paperback edition)
29. Prof Dr. Javed Iqbal Saani (2018) **Managerial Implications of the Battle of BADR**, Intellectual Capital Enterprise Limited, London, available on Amazon (Paperback edition)

Consolidations of significant themes

30. Prof Dr. Javed Iqbal Saani (2021) **Project Management: An Islamic Perspective**, Intellectual Capital Enterprise Limited, London, available on Amazon (Paperback edition)
31. Prof Dr. Javed Iqbal Saani (2018) **Management Practices of Prophet Muhammad (ﷺ)**, Intellectual Capital Enterprise Limited, London, available on Amazon (Paperback edition)
32. Prof Dr. Javed Iqbal Saani (2020) **Transformation Strategy of the Prophet (ﷺ) [PBUH]**, Intellectual Capital Enterprise Limited, London, available on Amazon (Paperback edition)
33. Prof Dr. Javed Iqbal Saani (2019) **Financial Management Strategy of the Prophet (ﷺ) (PBUH)**, Intellectual Capital Enterprise Limited, London, available on Amazon (Paperback edition)
34. Prof Dr. Javed Iqbal Saani (2019) **Information Management Strategy of the Prophet (ﷺ) (PBUH)**, Intellectual Capital Enterprise Limited, London, available on Amazon (Paperback edition)
35. Prof Dr. Javed Iqbal Saani (2019) **Motivation Strategy of the Prophet (ﷺ) (PBUH)**, Intellectual Capital Enterprise Limited, London, available on Amazon (Paperback edition)
36. Prof Dr. Javed Iqbal Saani (2019) **Strategic Management: The Approach of the Prophet (ﷺ) (PBUH)**, Intellectual Capital Enterprise Limited, London, available on Amazon (Paperback edition)

Identification of Managerial functions

37. Prof Dr. Javed Iqbal Saani (2018) **Managerial Thoughts of the Prophet (ﷺ),** Intellectual Capital Enterprise Limited, London, available on Amazon (Paperback edition)
38. Prof Dr. Javed Iqbal Saani (2018) **Controlling Strategy of the Prophet (ﷺ)**, Intellectual Capital Enterprise Limited, London, available on Amazon (Paperback edition)
39. Prof Dr. Javed Iqbal Saani (2018) **Leading Strategy of the Prophet (ﷺ)**, Intellectual Capital Enterprise Limited, London, available on Amazon (Paperback edition)
40. Prof Dr. Javed Iqbal Saani (2018) **Organising Strategy of the Prophet (ﷺ)**, Intellectual Capital Enterprise Limited, London, available on Amazon (Paperback edition)
41. Prof Dr. Javed Iqbal Saani (2018) **Planning Strategy of the Prophet (ﷺ)**, Intellectual Capital Enterprise Limited, London, available on Amazon (Paperback edition)
42. Prof Dr. Javed Iqbal Saani (2017) **Prophet Muhammad (ﷺ) as a planning expert**, available on Amazon (Paperback edition)

Specific topics

43. Prof Dr. Javed Iqbal Saani (2017) **Sales and Marketing: Selected Ahadith**, available on amazon.co.uk. (Paperback edition)
44. Prof Dr. Javed Iqbal Saani (2016) **Responsibilities of Managers: Selected Ahadith**, available on amazon.co.uk. (Paperback edition)

Management Sciences

1. Prof Dr. Javed Iqbal Saani (2019) Management Information Systems, Intellectual Capital Enterprise Limited, London, available on Amazon (Paperback edition)
2. Prof Dr. Javed Iqbal Saani (2018) Managing Your Projects, Intellectual Capital Enterprise Limited, London, available on amazon.co.uk. (Paperback edition)

3. Prof Dr. Javed Iqbal Saani (2017) Business Case Studies, Intellectual Capital Enterprise Limited, London, available on Amazon (Paperback edition)
4. Prof Dr. Prof Dr. Javed Iqbal Saani (2016) Research Proposals: Contents & Exemplars, available on amazon.co.uk. (Paperback edition)
5. Prof Dr. Javed Iqbal Saani (2012) Understanding Information Systems, Manchester: GRaASS.
6. Prof Dr Javed Iqbal Saani (2011) Digital Divide in South Asia, ISBN: 9789699578120.
7. Prof Dr. Javed Iqbal Saani and Muhammad Rafi Khattak (2011) Managing Risk in Projects, ISBN: 9789699578090.
8. Prof Dr. Javed Iqbal Saani and Muhammad Nadeem Khan (2011, 2018) Understanding Project Management, ISBN: 978969957845, available on Amazon (Paperback edition)
9. Prof Dr. Javed Iqbal Saani (2011) Information Systems for Managers, Grass Books, Manchester.
10. Prof Dr. Javed Iqbal Saani (2010) Managing strategic change: a real-world case study, ISBN: 978-3838330952, available on amazon.co.uk. (Paperback edition)

General Interest

1. Prof Dr. Javed Iqbal Saani (2021) **Key Topics in Islam**, Intellectual Capital Enterprise Limited, London, available on Amazon (Paperback & Kindle edition)
2. Prof Dr. Javed Iqbal Saani (2021) **Significance of Mosques in Islam**, Intellectual Capital Enterprise Limited, London, available on Amazon (Paperback edition)
3. Prof Dr. Javed Iqbal Saani (2021) **Rewards of Virtuous Deeds**, Intellectual Capital Enterprise Limited, London, available on Amazon (Paperback edition)
4. Prof Dr. Javed Iqbal Saani (2020) **Islamic Perspective of Knowledge**, Intellectual Capital Enterprise Limited, London, available on Amazon (Paperback edition)
5. Prof Dr. Javed Iqbal Saani (2019) The **Intercession of the Prophet (ﷺ)** (PBUH), Intellectual Capital Enterprise Limited, London, available on Amazon (Paperback edition)

6. Prof Dr. Javed Iqbal Saani (2019) **Who are Wrongdoers [Zalimoon]?** Intellectual Capital Enterprise Limited, London, available on Amazon (Paperback edition)
7. Prof Dr. Javed Iqbal Saani (2019) **Characteristics of Successful People**, Intellectual Capital Enterprise Limited, London, available on Amazon (Paperback edition)
8. Prof Dr. Javed Iqbal Saani (2019) **Key Campaigns of the Prophet [PBUH]**, Intellectual Capital Enterprise Limited, London, available on Amazon (Paperback edition)
9. Prof Dr. Javed Iqbal Saani (2019) **The Importance of Islamic Greeting**, Intellectual Capital Enterprise Limited, London, available on Amazon (Paperback edition)
10. Prof Dr. Javed Iqbal Saani (2019) **Who are Mujrimoon: Criminals, Polytheists & Sinners?** Intellectual Capital Enterprise Limited, London, available on Amazon (Paperback edition)
11. Prof Dr. Javed Iqbal Saani (2019) **GLAD TIDINGS of Allah (SWT) and His Apostle (PBUH) TO NOBLE PEOPLE**, Intellectual Capital Enterprise Limited, London, available on Amazon (Paperback edition)
12. Prof Dr. Javed Iqbal Saani (2019) **Qualities of Righteous People**, Intellectual Capital Enterprise Limited, London, available on Amazon (Paperback edition)
13. Prof Dr. Javed Iqbal Saani (2019) **Greatness of Allah (SWT) in the Words of Allah (SWT)**, Intellectual Capital Enterprise Limited, London, available on Amazon (Paperback edition)
14. Prof Dr. Javed Iqbal Saani (2019) **Tablighi Mazaakry: The Programme & Contents of the Work of Dawah**, Intellectual Capital Enterprise Limited, London, available on Amazon (Paperback edition)
15. Prof Dr. Javed Iqbal Saani (2018) **Qualities of Momins: The Quranic Perspective**, Intellectual Capital Enterprise Limited, London, available on Amazon (Paperback edition)
16. Prof Dr. Javed Iqbal Saani (2018) **Hajj Experience: Combining Dawah and Manasiks**, Intellectual Capital Enterprise Limited, London, available on Amazon (Paperback edition)

17. Prof Dr. Javed Iqbal Saani (2018) **Sukhn-e-Saani** (The book of poetry), Intellectual Capital Enterprise Limited, London, available on Amazon (Paperback edition)
18. Prof Dr. Javed Iqbal Saani (2017) **Virtues of Sickness: Selected Ahadith**, available on Amazon (Paperback edition)
19. Prof Dr. Javed Iqbal Saani (2017) **Muhammad (PBUH): His Trials & Tribulations**, available on Amazon (Paperback edition)
20. Prof Dr. Javed Iqbal Saani (2016) **Experience: The Journey of My Life**, available on amazon.co.uk. (Paperback edition)

Books translated into Arabic.

1- النبي محمّد (ﷺ) وتطور نظرية الإدارة تأليف البروفيسور جاويد إقبال ثاني ترجمة البروفيسور الحبيب ثابتي

Prophet (ﷺ) Muhammad [PBUH] & Evolution of Management Theory, translated by Professor Al-Habib Thabiti, University of Mascara, Algeria.

2- تعلُّم الفقار الإدارية من القرآن الكريم تأليف البروفيسور جاويد إقبال ثاني ترجمة البروفيسور الحبيب ثابتي

Learning of Managerial Ideas from Quran, translated by Professor Al-Habib Thabiti, University of Mascara, Algeria.

3- الممارسات الإدارية للنبي محمد صلى الله عليه وسلم تأليف البروفيسور جاويد إقبال ثاني ترجمة البروفيسور الحبيب ثابتي

Management Practices of Prophet Muhammad (ﷺ) translated by Professor Al-Habib Thabiti, University of Mascara, Algeria.

4- ريادة العمال من منظور إسلامي تأليف البروفيسور جاويد إقبال ثاني ترجمة البروفيسور الحبيب ثابتي

Islamic Perspective of Entrepreneurship, translated by Professor Al-Habib Thabiti, University of Mascara, Algeria.

5- إدارة المشاريع من منظور إسلامي تأليف البروفيسور جاويد إقبال ثاني ترجمة البروفيسور الحبيب ثابتي

Project Management: An Islamic Perspective, translated by Professor Al-Habib Thabiti, University of Mascara, Algeria.

6- مقدمة في نظرية الإدارة الإسلامية تأليف البروفيسور جاويد إقبال ثاني ترجمة البروفيسور الحبيب ثابتي

Introduction to Islamic Management Theory, translated by Professor Al-Habib Thabiti, University of Mascara, Algeria.

7- مبادئ الإدارة الإسلامية تأليف البروفيسور جاويد إقبال ثاني ترجمة البروفيسور الحبيب ثابتي

Principles of Islamic Management, translated by Professor Al-Habib Thabiti, University of

Mascara, Algeria.

8- كيف اكتشفت نظرية الإدارة الإسلامية؟ تأليف البروفيسور جاويد إقبال ثاني ترجمة البروفيسور الحبيب ثابتي

How I have Discovered Islamic Management Theory? translated by Professor Al-Habib Thabiti, University of Mascara, Algeria.

REFERENCES

[1] https://www.collinsdictionary.com/dictionary/english/crisis

[2] Synonym study: Danger, hazard, peril, jeopardy imply harm that one may encounter. Danger is the general word for liability to all kinds of injury or evil consequences, either near at hand and certain, or remote and doubtful: to be in danger of being killed.

Hazard suggests a danger that one can foresee but cannot avoid: A mountain climber is exposed to many hazards. Peril usually denotes great and imminent danger: The passengers on the disabled ship were in great peril. Jeopardy, a less common word, has essentially the same meaning as peril, but emphasizes exposure to the chances of a situation: To save his friend he put his life in jeopardy. Source: https://www.dictionary.com/browse/danger

[3] https://www.merriamwebster.com/dictionary/difficulty

[4] https://www.yourdictionary.com/difficulty

[5] https://www.yourdictionary.com/problem

[6] https://www.pagecentertraining.psu.edu/public-relations-ethics/ethics-in-crisis-management/lesson-1-prominent-ethical-issues-in-crisis-situations/crisis-and-crisis-management/

[7] https://www.pagecentertraining.psu.edu/public-relations-ethics/ethics-in-crisis-management/lesson-1-prominent-ethical-issues-in-crisis-situations/crisis-and-crisis-management/

[8] Boundy, J., Michael D. Pfarrer, Cole E. Short and W. Timothy Coombs, (2017) Crises and Crisis Management: Integration, Interpretation, and Research Development, *Journal of Management*, Vol. 43 No. 6, July 2017, 1661–1692; DOI: 10.1177/0149206316680030.

[9] https://www.smartsheet.com/content/crisis-management-model-theories? amp

[10] Kreitner, p. 48.

[11] Iqbal Saani, Javed (2020) Prophet (ﷺ) Muhammad [PBUH] & Evolution of Management Theory, Intellectual Capital Enterprise Limited, London, available on Amazon (Paperback edition)

[12] Mitroff, I.I. (1994). Crisis management and environmentalism: A natural fit., California Management Review, 36(2), pp. 101-113.

[13] https://www.dictionary.com/browse/danger

[14] https://www.smartsheet.com/content/crisis-management-model-theories? amp

[15] Boundy, J., Michael D. Pfarrer, Cole E. Short and W. Timothy Coombs, (2017) Crises and Crisis Management: Integration, Interpretation, and Research Development, *Journal of Management*, Vol. 43 No. 6, July 2017, 1661–1692; DOI: 10.1177/0149206316680030.

[16] Mubarikpuri, p. 69.

[17] Sahih al-Bukhari 1871; In-book reference: Book 29, Hadith 5.

[18] Kaandhlawi (2012), v. p.339.

[19] Lings, 317.

[20] Mubarakpuri, Safiur Rahman (1995) "The Sealed Nectar" (Ar-Raheeq Al-Makhtum), Lahore: Al-Maktba Alsalfia. P. 311.

[21] Pearson, Christine M and Mitroff, Ian I (1993) From crisis prone to crisis prepared: A framework for crisis management, The Executive; 7, 1; pp. 48-59.

[22] Pearson, Christine M and Mitroff, Ian I (1993) From crisis prone to crisis prepared: A framework for crisis management, *The Executive*; 7, 1; pp. 48-59.

[23] Mubarikpuri, P. 246.

[24] Mubarikpuri, P. 200.

[25] Lings, p. 317.

[26] Siddiqi, p. 415 (Urdu edition).

[27] Iqbal Saani, Javed (2019) Managerial Implications of the Major Expeditions of the Prophet (ﷺ) [PBUH], Intellectual Capital Enterprise Limited, London, available on Amazon (Paperback edition)

[28] Kandhelvi, Molana Yousaf P. 374.

[29] P. 85, The English Translation.

[30] Kaandhlawi (2012), p.341.

[31] Lings, p. 114.

[32] Iqbal Saani, Javed (2019) Managerial Implications of the Major Expeditions of the Prophet (ﷺ) [PBUH], Intellectual Capital Enterprise Limited, London, available on Amazon (Paperback edition)

[33] Mubarikpuri, P. 579.

[34] Lings, P. 318.

[35] https://languages.oup.com/google-dictionary-en/

[36] Mubarikpuri, p. 311-12.

[37] Mubarikpuri, p. 313.

[38] Lings, p. 216.

[39] Hijazi, Abu Tariq (2012) Hudaibiyah: A turning point in the history of Islam, http://www.arabnews.com/hudaibiyah-turning-point-history-islam

[40] Lings, p. 247.

[41] Mobarikpuri, p. 462.

[42] Pearson, Christine M and Mitroff, Ian I (1993) From crisis prone to crisis prepared: A framework for crisis management, The Executive; 7, 1; pp. 48-59.

[43] Mubarikpuri, p. 389-92 [Urdu edition].

[44] Ibn Ishaq, p. 545.

[45] Lings, p. 297.

[46] Mobarikpuri, p. 492-93.

[47] Mobarikpuri, p. 492-93.

[48] Lings, p. 299.

[49] https://www.yourdictionary.com/recovery

[50] Lings, p. 249.

[51] Iqbal Saani, Javed (2019) Managerial Implications of the Major Expeditions of the Prophet (ﷺ) [PBUH], Intellectual Capital Enterprise Limited, London, available on Amazon (Paperback edition)

[52] Ibn Ishaq, p. 504.

[53] Lings, p. 254-55.

[54] Iqbal Saani, Javed (2019) Managerial Implications of the Major Expeditions of the Prophet (ﷺ) [PBUH], Intellectual Capital Enterprise Limited, London, available on Amazon (Paperback edition)

[55] Saani, Iqbal Javed (2019) Managerial Thoughts of the Prophet [PBUH], Intellectual Capital Enterprise Limited, London, available on amazon (Paperback edition)

[56] Iqbal Saani, Javed (2019) Managerial Implications of the Major Expeditions of the Prophet (ﷺ) [PBUH], Intellectual Capital Enterprise Limited, London, available on Amazon (Paperback edition)

[57] Mobarikpuri, pp. 262-63.

[58] Ibn Ishaq, p. 386-87.

[59] Lings, pp. 195-96.

[60] Christine, Pearson M and Mitroff, Ian I (1993) From crisis prone to crisis prepared: A framework for crisis management, The Executive; 7, 1.

[61] Christine, Pearson M and Mitroff, Ian I (1993) From crisis prone to crisis prepared: A framework for crisis management, The Executive; 7, 1; p. 54.

[62] Sahih al-Bukhari 4210; In-book reference: Book 64, Hadith 250.

[63] Lings, p. 249.

[64] Mobarikpuri, pp. 339-40.

[65] 20. Iqbal Javed and Muhammad Mushtaq Ahmad (2009) Planning in the Islamic Tradition: The Case of Hijrah Expedition, INSIGHT, Vol.1, No. 3, pp. 37-68.

[66] Ibn Ishaq, p. 223.

[67] Ibn Ishaq, p. 223.

[68] Iqbal Saani, Javed (2018) Managerial Implications of the Hijrah Expedition, Intellectual Capital Enterprise Limited, London, available on Amazon (Paperback edition)

[69] Sahih al-Bukhari 3922; in-book reference : Book 63, Hadith 147.

[70] Lings, p. 119.

71 Ibn Ishaq, p. 225-26.

72 Kandhelvi, Molana Yousaf, P. 130.

73 Mubarikpuri, p. 158-59.

74 Mubarikpuri, p. 161.

75 Ibn Ishaq, p. 192.

76 Iqbal Saani, Javed (2019) Information Management Strategy of the Prophet (ﷺ) (PBUH), Intellectual Capital Enterprise Limited, London, available on Amazon (Paperback edition)

77 Mubarikpuri, p. 340 (Urdu edition).

78 Shibli & Noamani, V. 1, p. 270.

79 Phalwarvi, p. 503.

80 Mobarikpuri, pp. 592.

81 Mobarikpuri, pp. 394.

82 Mobarikpuri, pp. 301-2.

83. Lings, p. 216.

84 Shibli & Noamani, V. 1, p. 225 (Urdu edition).

85 Lings, p. 173-74.

86 The chapter is associated with the battle of Uhad.

[87] The model of analysis in this chapter is different from the rest of the book because it was written earlier without application of a model.

[88] https://www.collinsdictionary.com/dictionary/english/crisis

[89] Synonym study: Danger, hazard, peril, jeopardy imply harm that one may encounter. Danger is the general word for liability to all kinds of injury or evil consequences, either near at hand and certain, or remote and doubtful: to be in danger of being killed.

Hazard suggests a danger that one can foresee but cannot avoid: A mountain climber is exposed to many hazards. Peril usually denotes great and imminent danger: The passengers on the disabled ship were in great peril. Jeopardy, a less common word, has essentially the same meaning as peril, but emphasizes exposure to the chances of a situation: To save his friend he put his life in jeopardy. Source: https://www.dictionary.com/browse/danger

[90] https://www.merriamwebster.com/dictionary/difficulty

[91] https://www.yourdictionary.com/difficulty

[92] https://www.yourdictionary.com/problem

[93] Mobarikpuri 1995.

[94] P. 349.

[95] Harrington, K (2017) 6 ways to handle a PR crisis, https://www.ragan.com/6-ways-to-handle-a-prcrisis/

[96] Kenton, K (2017) Crisis Management, https://www.investopedia.com/terms/c/crisismanagement.asp

[97] P. 172.

[98] P. 172.

[99] Saani, Iqbal Javed (2019) Managerial Thoughts of the Prophet [PBUH], Intellectual Capital Enterprise Limited, London, available on amazon (Paperback edition)

[100] Mubarikpuri, p. 340-41.

[101] Lings, p. 173.

[102] P. 166-67.

[103] Mitroff, I.I. (1994). Crisis management and environmentalism: A natural fit., California Management Review, 36(2), pp. 101-113.

[104] Pangarkar, Nitin (2016) A framework for effective crisis response, Journal of Organizational Change Management, Vol. 29, No. 4, pp. 464-483.

[105] Mansoorpuri, v. 2, pp. 151.

[106] Iqbal Saani, Javed (2019) Information Management Strategy of the Prophet (ﷺ) (PBUH), Intellectual Capital Enterprise Limited, London, available on Amazon (Paperback edition)

[107] Mitroff, I.I. (1994). Crisis management and environmentalism: A natural fit., California Management Review, 36(2), pp. 101-113.

[108] Pangarkar, Nitin (2016) A framework for effective crisis response, Journal of Organizational Change Management, Vol. 29, No. 4, pp. 464-483.

138

Notes

www.ingramcontent.com/pod-product-compliance
Lightning Source LLC
Chambersburg PA
CBHW060417220526
45465CB00008B/2915